REMARKABLE JOURNEYS OF THE
SECOND WORLD WAR

REMARKABLE JOURNEYS OF THE
SECOND WORLD WAR

A Collection of Untold Stories

COMPILED BY

VICTORIA PANTON BACON

First published 2020

The History Press
97 St George's Place, Cheltenham,
Gloucestershire, GL50 3QB
www.thehistorypress.co.uk

British Library Cataloguing in Publication Data.
A catalogue record for this book is available from the British Library.

ISBN 978 0 7509 9486 6

Typesetting and origination by The History Press
Printed and bound by Imak, Turkey.

To the thousands, upon thousands, of men and women who deserve our thanks and remembrance, as much as those who have told their stories for this book.

To all who gave us our freedom.

CONTENTS

ENDORSEMENTS

JOANNA LUMLEY OBE, Actress and Campaigner

History is made up of billions of shards of experiences, each valuable and essential to make up the larger picture, each tiny yet all-important at the same time. In this fascinating and touching book we hear from survivors of the Second World War in their own words. Their very personal accounts of this huge and terrible period of history show courage, humour, pity and horror, splinters of memory, glittering and vital to our understanding of war, and its effects on those who lived through it.

**TERRY WAITE CBE, Former Beirut Hostage and
Humanitarian Campaigner**

I happen to be one of the diminishing number of those who were born just before the outbreak of the Second World War. I still have vivid memories of a fighter plane crash-landing in the road beside our house and of soldiers marching in formation along the road towards their barracks. At night my mother was careful to cover all the windows with blackout material so that we would not be spotted by enemy aircraft.

Those men and women who actually took an active part in combat are increasingly few in number and they have even more vivid memories.

Victoria has performed a valuable service in recording their experiences in this book. Not only has she provided the reader with a fascinating account of those years, but she has given us a unique insight into the lives of some of those who left their homes and occupations and entered a strange new world. She covers a wide territory from the Home Guard to Burma to Bomber Command and Auschwitz.

There is little glamour in warfare. It is brutal, frightening and horrible. It is important that we remember those years not only to pay tribute to those who gave their lives but also to remind ourselves that we owe it to future generations to do all in our power to promote peace and harmony in this world.

JONATHAN DIMBLEBY, Broadcaster and Historian

This collection of the Second World War memories is a gem. The front-line stories are humane, modest and compassionate – inspiring admiration to the point of awe.

SIMON PEARSON, Author and Obituaries Editor of *The Times*

People sometimes forget that war is not about cold metal – aircraft, battleships and tanks. It is about the pain and suffering of human beings, their courage and anxieties, and the relationships that generate hope and fear. In *Remarkable Journeys of the Second*

World War, Victoria Panton Bacon captures the vulnerability of the human spirit – at sea, on land and in the air, from the Lancaster navigator watching the stars; to the wine waiter on the high seas; the young Hungarian Jew who made a life after Auschwitz; and the warrior historian seeking truth. Her book is full of remarkable testimony, a series of remarkable journeys.

JOSHUA LEVINE, Second World War Author and Historian

As the Second World War passes from living memory, Victoria presents an extraordinary cast of characters who reveal what it was like to take part in the fight for freedom. From cavalrymen to rear gunners to merchant seamen, this book reveals the partic- ipants as human beings with recognisable passions and emotions. Their stories are exciting, heart-breaking and vitally important.

TED WILSON, Author and Veteran of the Vietnam War

Victoria Panton Bacon has woven together voices with histori- cal context to create the Bayeux Tapestry of the Second World War. An important part of her book is her own perspective as someone who is two generations separated from those who lived through the trauma. For those of my own generation, Baby Boomers born in the 1940s, the men and women who experienced the war were parents, teachers and work colleagues. We often sat next to them in staff rooms and saw them on a daily basis. In some ways, we took them for granted and did not fully appreciate what they had experienced. Victoria is from the grandchild generation and the freshness of her perspective is a vital part of this book. If anything, she has taught us that we should love these extraordinary men and women even more than we do.

Remarkable Journeys of the Second World War is an outstanding book which deserves to become a classic of the period. Victoria's narrative gets up close and personal to her truly remarkable interviewees. Her sympathy for and interaction with these individuals creates honest and gripping revelations. The voices in this book reflect a wide range of war experience. There are pilots, sailors, Home Guard soldiers, POWs – and the harrowing recollections of a Bergen–Belsen survivor (an account that should be read in history lessons in every school).

Although much has been written about this period, Victoria constantly turns over new leaves. Far from the *Dad's Army* image of popular imagination, the Home Guard suffered 1,206 killed. In addition to the horrors of the gas ovens, there was also the sadistic twist of having family photos confiscated by concentration camp guards – sadism that becomes emotional as well as physical.

I must also praise the writing skill and professionalism with which this book has been woven together. Each voice is unique and utterly memorable. At times tragic, at times humorous, but always gripping, *Remarkable Journeys of the Second World War* is a book that will reverberate in the reader's mind long after the final page.

FOREWORD
BY ELIZABETH HALLS

(Author of her Father's Second World War Diary,
Flying Blind: The Story of a Second World War
Night Fighter Pilot)

When I looked it up to check, I was surprised to find that the last surviving service veteran of the First World War was not 'the last fighting Tommy', Harry Patch (1898–2009) as I had thought: he was the last surviving veteran to have fought in the trenches; nor was it Claude Choules (1901–2011), a British Australian who was the last surviving combatant, and who served in the Royal Navy in both world wars. It was, in fact, a lady called Florence Green, who joined the Women's Royal Air Force when she was just 17, in the summer of 1918.

The WRAF had been formed a few months earlier, so that women could do jobs such as mechanics, cooks and clerks, thus freeing up more men for active service. Florence never saw combat. Her wartime memories were of the base at RAF Marham, where she waited at tables as a mess steward, and the pilots she met, admired and sometimes dated. When she died in Norfolk in 2012, aged 110, it was the humble Florence who represented the ending of her era.

I mention this because it so clearly highlights the fact that the two world wars involved not only, and not even mainly, professional combatants, but volunteers and 'ordinary' people, both men and women, and directly affected people of all ages, including children, in all walks of life.

Victoria's collection of memories from the Second World War reflects this fact. It is not so much a memoir of a war as the recording of another disappearing era by those who still survive. This book does not concentrate on the battles, the manoeuvres, the aircraft, the ships and the tanks: the progress of the conflict. Instead, it looks at individual lives and lets them be the lens through which we gain an understanding not principally of the war itself, or how it was won, but of what it was like to live it. And in the process, as we see the individual spirit, courage and resilience of each person's tale, set against the sadness and the struggle from which they rose, we realise something profound about why the winning happened, against all the odds.

We are also invited, as we read, to accompany Victoria on her own remarkable journey as she interviews her subjects. Unusually, for a series of memoirs, Victoria herself appears in the pages in relation to the veterans and their unfolding stories. We are sometimes there with her in the room, and she becomes for us an 'Everyman' of our own age, as she reaches back to try and understand what it was like for them to live their own life in wartime. In this, the book is a journey for all of us.

I embarked on my own remarkable journey in 2012 when, after my father, ex–Flight Lieutenant Bryan Wild died aged 90, I discovered his diaries, photographs and unfinished memoirs of his time as a fighter pilot during the Second World War. Like Victoria with her grandfather's writings, I had the joy and privilege of compiling and editing my father's memoirs, published as *Flying Blind: The Story of a Second World War Night Fighter Pilot* in 2014, by Fonthill Media. The researching and writing of that book took me on my own emotional journey into my father's memory, connecting me deeply with the young man he was then – not a part of him I ever knew in life – and immersing me in a knowledge of that wartime period I never thought to have. The next year, on a crazy impulse, I sold my modern 4 x 4 in order to buy a 1936 Singer Le Mans sports car of the same make, model and colour as my father's favourite car, one he bought in 1944 from a fellow pilot. In 2015, raising funds and profile for the RAF Benevolent Fund, I took it to all sixty airfields on the British mainland where he landed during the war, a remarkable journey indeed that was more amazing to me than words can say – I met relatives of my father's wartime friends.

I discovered that every airfield had its own surprise and gift. And in Norfolk, one of those was meeting Victoria, with whom a warm correspondence had grown around a shared experience of connection with that wartime era and a sense of duty to record and remember what was handed to us. The five short stories written by her grandfather, which are included in this book, are part of her own family inheritance.

Why is it important to remember? Because, like Victoria's grandfather and my father, the war history is made up of individual lives; ordinary men and women like us, who lived and served and, in so many cases, died under the burden of conflict, each in their own allotted place and in their own unique way.

We live in their legacy. So, before the last one of them passes away, we listen, and remember to say, 'Thank you'.

That is what this book is all about.

Elizabeth Halls

FOREWORD BY LIEUTENANT GENERAL JAMES BASHALL

Come Together
Join Together
Remember Together

These words encapsulate the spirit of the work of the Royal British Legion, for which I am so proud and honoured to be president. We provide lifelong support to serving, and ex-serving, personnel and their families. We have been here since 1921 and we will be here as long as we are needed.

In 2020, the year in which *Remarkable Journeys of the Second World War* is published, we have been paying a special tribute to the men and women who served during the Second World War. Although our remembrance activities will be much reduced by the impact of Covid-19, we wish to celebrate the lives of those veterans still with us, and remember once more the freedoms and peace they secured for us.

The Second World War is important for many reasons. It was a conflict involving most of the world, and was partly born of the unsettled issues facing our global society since the Great War, now known as the First World War. Lasting from 1939 to 1945 and responsible for the horrors of the Holocaust, and the deaths of somewhere between 40 and 50 million people. Those who served in those years are now mostly in their late 90s. Soon, we'll have no living witnesses to the terrifying and triumphant events of a war that changed the world forever. The people who lived through those times – both military and civilian – deserve our recognition and to be remembered.

Victoria's book is therefore extremely important. These are real stories of real people from a range of backgrounds from across the globe, all of whom were caught up in the kaleidoscope of a war of national survival. We can learn so much from these stories. They remind us particularly of the human nature of conflict and its impact on ordinary lives; and as a veteran myself, the remarkable military journeys stand to inspire the next generation. It is in everyone's best interest to understand the events of the Second World War so we can prevent it happening again, and we need to cherish the memories of those who lived through those years – while we still can.

Victoria has written up these vital memories in a matter of fact manner, almost as if they are not real stories. But they are, and the chapters include stories from events that are little documented or known about. It is a remarkable book about a remarkable group of men and women, whose stories needed to be told.

We will remember them.

PREFACE

Every year, on 11 November, the pain of war is thrust into the forefront of our thinking. Through the wearing of poppies, laying of wreaths and singing of military hymns, we are encouraged to remember those who have suffered – and are still suffering – through conflict; those who have helped deliver the peace we have today.

I think it is absolutely right we are asked to 'remember them', and in doing so, acknowledge the physical and emotional pain of so many. However, in order to give this act of remembrance justice, we do need to understand. For a human being to empathise with the pain of another without having experienced that pain is challenging; some would argue, impossible. But, if we take the trouble to listen to or read of the experience we want to comprehend, our understanding of that situation can be deepened.

Therefore, I urge anyone who yearns for an appreciation of the Second World War, beyond knowledge of facts and figures, to read the testimonies in this book. Each chapter is a previously untold memory of the Second World War which shines a bright light on these six, dark years; illuminating the courage, actions and sentiments of thousands – millions – whose wartime experience changed the course of history.

The veterans who have recalled their memories for *Remarkable Journeys* have had to be brave, yet again, to cast their minds back over seventy years; but they have done so because they want to. Not only for themselves, but far more so, I am sure, for their friends and comrades who have not – or simply could not – do what they have done.

There is much sadness in this book, which you would expect of course, such as the awfulness that Piers de Bernière-Smart describes when being sent into battle (as a member of the Household Cavalry) after reconnaissance had been done that predicted horrifying loss, and the shock experienced by John Ottewell who cleared up carnage after the bombing of a Sunday school that killed, among others, twenty-six children.

However, there are surprises too – for example, Bill Carter told me how his love of music helped him through the war; Pat Rorke explained how Rudyard Kipling's poem 'If' aided her sanity in coping with the secrecy rules she was bound to obey while working in the unit handling Enigma code messages, and Douglas Huke, as a member of the Merchant Navy, who travelled all the way to Australia, told me he returned not with prisoners or soldiers, but only with a cargo of skinned rabbits.

When I read all of these chapters, which I am so privileged to have had the opportunity to write, I think how extraordinary they would be if they were fiction. But they are not fiction. They are fact. They illustrate the reality of war; nothing can better help us understand the Second World War than personal testimonies such as these.

Writing up these memories has been a 'remarkable journey' for me. I have been warmly welcomed into the homes of each veteran; there have been tears (sometimes mine) and laughs, but above all a searing honesty that has opened my eyes and deepened my understanding.

My journey began in 2012, after I came across my grandfather's handwritten memoir of the Second World War; the words of which – for fear of sounding trite – when I deciphered them, leapt off the page. His words transported me to France, as it was falling into occupation, in 1940.

My grandfather, Alastair Panton's, story is called *Six Weeks of Blenheim Summer*. It is his account of flying a Bristol Blenheim aircraft during the Battle of France in 1940. This was published two years after I found it, and has since been reprinted[1]. Many who have read it have thanked me for bringing it to fruition as the clarity of his writing has deepened their understanding of what it was to be part of the war, at a time when we were staring defeat in the face. It has also – to my delight – given many pause for thought about what their own family members possibly went through.

Finding the handwritten manuscript of *Blenheim Summer*, which was totally unexpected, among my own father's model aircraft after he died, marked the start of my own 'remarkable journey'. So, *Remarkable Journeys of the Second World War* is a sequel to *Blenheim Summer*; it is the continuation of my quest to deliver a deeper understanding of the Second World War to others through the writing up of true, personal testimonies which I have been so privileged to be given.

I hope by turning the pages of this book, you will have a 'remarkable journey' of your own.

---

1   Published by Biteback and Penguin respectively, 2014 and 2018.

Finally, in the words of Fred Howard, a friend of Peter Blackburn (Chapter 9):

We must all be grateful to the people who gave us this rich gift of their memories. They take us into a period of British history that those who lived in those dark days hoped never to have to go through again – but they were revolutionary times that altered the culture of rural England and the destiny of the nation.

Victoria Panton Bacon

1

NAVIGATION BY THE STARS – JOHN OTTEWELL

John was a navigator on Lancaster bombers. Here, he tells about the complexity of navigation, and of some of the humanitarian operations he took part in.

John Alan Ottewell, *c.* 1944. This shows Dad 'ready for action'.
(Chris Ottewell)

Lancaster Crew, 1944. (Chris Ottewell)

John Ottewell wanted to fly for as long as he could remember. One of his earliest memories was of being caught jumping off his parents' porch roof, holding an umbrella to use as a parachute. Upon learning this, I conjured up an image of a slightly naughty, gung-ho young boy doing something rather unadvisable. Landing in the uncomfortable heap that he did after his exploit with the umbrella could have put him off flying for good – but it didn't. That 'flight' might have been reckless, but he learned what it was like to be up high, look down and – fleetingly – be in the air rather than on the ground. It took courage to jump off that roof and, in spite of the pain of landing, his determination to be an airman was not diminished.

It was this enthusiasm that led him – and thousands like him – to the recruiting office of the Royal Air Force. John's memories made me think about how these young men must have felt as they signed up to be part of the Second World War. How nervous they must have been, but excited too – lives suddenly full of purpose and meaning, knowing that they were doing this for their country, and for the king.

'Pathfinder Crew' is a genuine period shot taken by an unknown person using Dad's Kodak camera. (Chris Ottewell)

Suddenly, in uniform, from what I have gleaned from the veterans to whom I have spoken for this book, upon joining their unit – be it army, RAF or navy – new recruits were so proud that the risks and dangers that war presented were secondary to the thrill of being accepted as part of the team. It was an enormous team, all with the same aim – at all costs, to win the war. I have to think at this point, though, of those they left behind. As they marched forward, those who remained could only stand still and wait. Every day as the war progressed, new recruits were nervously waved off to begin their journey by mothers, fathers, grandparents, brothers, sisters, cousins, friends and lovers.

Those left behind stood tall with pride, but it almost hurts as I write this to think of the fear of loss that their hearts must have also been pierced with. Of course, we can be certain of nothing, such is human nature, but war creates a level of vulnerability that is hard perhaps to comprehend, unless we have been there. It creates

The occasion when John met his tail gunner in January 2018 (appropriately, he really was called Charlie!) for the first time since 1945. (Chris Ottewell)

a situation where life can be snatched away at any moment, and every day when it isn't, is a gift. This is true, of course, for all of us, all of the time, but the consciousness of that must be heightened in war. The vulnerability felt by those fighting and those who remain behind can create inner strength that may be empowering, but at the same time, such vulnerability could be overwhelming if one allowed a fear of dying to prevail.

Flying Officer John Ottewell began his basic training with the RAF after signing up when he reached the minimum age of 18. Once into his training the painful reality of war soon hit him, hard. Two bombs fell dangerously close to him, wreaking the carnage the enemy had planned for them. It happened while he was doing physical training on a beach at Babbacombe in Devon, on 30 May in 1943. While drilling, he and his fellow trainees – around twenty young men – suddenly heard a roaring noise. They looked out towards the direction of the sound and saw a German FW

John as a cheeky 6-year-old (approx.). (Chris Ottewell)

(Focke Wulf) 190 fighter aircraft flying low towards them, so as to be under the radar. Within moments it had dropped both of the bombs it was carrying.

The first bomb, said John, tore through the top of the hotel where they were billeted. It went from 'front to back', he recalled, causing a lot of damage and destroying the personal kit he had just been issued. This same bomb eventually went through the house behind the hotel and was dealt with by bomb-disposal experts.

It was the second bomb, however, that resulted in the havoc and suffering. It took the lives of thirty people that afternoon – twenty-six of them children. It landed on a village hall in nearby St Marychurch, while Sunday school was taking place. It was 'terrible', said John. 'It all happened in a matter of moments. We heard the bomb and it was soon followed by clouds of paper floating down, onto the beach.' These were the pages of hymn books,

John said, ironically revealing words of praise, forgiveness and courage. John and his comrades went as soon as they could to the scene of the devastation.

Words from the Gospel of Matthew are inscribed on the memorial stone that has been erected near the site of the bombing, to remember those who died, 'Blessed are the pure in heart, for they shall see God [Matthew 5.8]'. I hope their suffering was short and their last few moments peaceful. It is those who are left behind who subsequently suffer the most.

John Ottewell's description of what happened that day was very vivid. Since our conversation, an image has been imprinted in my mind of a group of young men on a beach, on a warm sunny day, quietly marching and enjoying the camaraderie – the reality of war still far away. Then suddenly, their peace was shattered. In an instant they were vulnerable, the war had become real. Drilling, marching, teamwork skills – what they were learning probably took on a whole new meaning. There was sudden reasoning behind the orders they were under pressure to obey, and a sense of urgency would, I think, have gripped them. A realisation that the job for which they were being trained was the most important in the world. Lives depended upon their diligence, dedication and – most of all – success. Witnessing the hideous killing and maiming of human beings – particularly those so young, with their lives ahead of them – was not something that could be tolerated.

The Babbacombe bombing took place in May 1943, almost seventy-five years before John Ottewell spoke to me about it. The years may have dulled the initial shock of what he witnessed, but the sadness has clearly remained with him. It was quite exhausting for him to describe this to me. Indeed, it was draining for me even to take it in.

This was the beginning of the Second World War for John Ottewell. It was important that he told me this – and it is why it matters for veterans to tell us their memories because there are, tragically, many accounts such as this; a huge number of significant life-changing battles and happenings that have gone virtually unrecorded, and if not spoken of, are forgotten.

However, after moving on from the sadness of Babbacombe, John lifted the mood with much talk about his job in the war, that of being a navigator on the mighty Lancaster bomber. It was with justifiable pride that he described the skills required and the instruments used. For his abilities and recorded successes, he is the recipient of not only a Distinguished Flying Medal (DFM), but also a Légion d'honneur.

Again, John's words put pictures in my head. Throughout this part of our conversation I felt almost transported to the cockpit of the Lancaster, sitting, slightly squashed, maps askew, on a stool facing buttons, levers and knobs on a panel displaying numbers and needle gauges which were swinging from left to right. It would have been a cockpit choked with courage, conscientiousness and responsibility. Each and every sortie they undertook was a perilous operation. One of a seven-man crew, John was seated in the cockpit behind the pilot – he was the guide, while the pilot was the driver. The others, with equally important roles to play, were in their hands.

After training, John Ottewell joined 115 Squadron, a main-force Lancaster squadron, which took him to such places as Normandy and the Ruhr. During the Second World War, 115 Squadron's base moved five times, but always remained in East Anglia.

John was particularly friendly with the rear gunner, their own 'Tail End Charlie', who was appropriately called Charlie (Sargeant), and the mid-upper gunner, also called Charlie (Shepherd.) When not on operations, John and 'the Charlies' would often cycle to the nearest town for a break and to recharge their batteries. Sometimes they would have a flutter in a betting shop, and in 1944 this resulted in them nicknaming their own Lancaster 'Tehran' after successfully betting that a horse of that name would win the famous St Leger horse race, which to this day still takes place annually in Doncaster. Such was his fondness for the Lancaster and crew that, at the time, John made a model of it, decorating it with the names of the crew.

Respect for aeroplanes was a common thread, I discovered, through my conversations with all the RAF veterans. Perhaps for them to feel their plane was the safest, strongest and most robust was a wonderful thing – a sort of emotional security blanket. John Ottewell was clearly very thankful that he had been able to go through the war in a Lancaster – it was probably the aircraft that most RAF trainees ultimately hoped they would fly in and many of them did because it was the RAF's principal heavy bomber, at least during the latter half of the war. It was also one of the largest aircraft. Powered by four engines that drove four sets of propellers, it was capable of flying even if two of its engines were lost, and its size and durability meant it carried the largest bombs – some weighing up to 12,000lb (5,400kg) – in addition to other, smaller incendiaries.

John's pride in being in a Lancaster crew was matched by my grandfather, Alastair Panton who flew Bristol Blenheims at the beginning of the war. Even though Alastair's battle days were cut short with his capture by the Germans in July 1940 after crash-landing his aircraft, he nonetheless had a deep respect for it. He wrote, 'The affection and trust I had developed for my Blenheim under normal conditions became wondering admiration throughout the six week campaign of the Battle of France.' Such affection was matched by Colin Bell, who piloted the 'Wooden Wonder' – a de Havilland Mosquito – fifty times over Germany, evading many determined attacks of the enemy (Colin's story is in Chapter 7).

Having survived his first tour of duty, during which he was awarded the Distinguished Flying Medal (DFM), John Ottewell and most of his crew volunteered to go directly on to a second tour, this time in the elite Pathfinder Force. They joined 7 Squadron, and he was promoted from the position of Flight Sergeant to Flying Officer.

Pathfinders were tasked with the responsibility of dropping coloured makers on targets for the following main-force bombers, indicating where they should drop their bombs if the targets were obscured by cloud. They did this by releasing flares which ignited and burned under parachutes as they slowly descended from about 1,000ft above the clouds. The main bomber aircraft then used these as an aiming point, correcting for wind and altitude, in order to try and hit a target they couldn't see.

The Pathfinders' job was to drop the flares as accurately as possible, and in all raids there would have been a 'Master Bomber' whose job it was to keep an eye on the markers (which might drift quite rapidly in the wind) and call for new markers as required, while informing the main-force bombers which markers to use and which to ignore. It was a technique called 'Wanganui' – it was very difficult, particularly in the wind. John knew that misplaced flares would have led to misplaced bombs, and misplaced bombs could lead to civilian lives destroyed. They did their best, but of course the scene was already set. This was war.

So, to navigation. There is no doubt, and John certainly did not pretend otherwise, that the task of guiding huge aircraft from A to B, often in darkness, in skies busy with the enemy, was extremely challenging. Even with the introduction of radar, which arrived in the early part of the war, intense levels of concentration and attention to detail were continually required.

Accuracy was essential in the meeting of objectives on the first occasion as failure could not only result in the loss of civilian life but also, for John and his crew, in having to return to the same target to finish the job. John explained to me how, without today's radio aids and GPS systems, navigators had to rely on their charts, two watches, their compass and a sextant to navigate across the dark skies of Europe to find a target that might well be camouflaged or disguised by the use of a 'clever' dummy target nearby. But, said John, 'German decoy flares and markers never quite matched those dropped by the Allies' red, green and orange markers.'

He explained to me:

The sextant was very similar to the type that sailors have used for centuries; but because aircraft move much faster than ships it was difficult to take an accurate star altitude, by that I mean taking an angle with the horizon. It had a bubble like a spirit level, and a little clockwork mechanism which gave an average of six shots, resulting in the altitude appearing on the counter, and a hook on the top that hung in a dome.

John told me that 'later versions had a more complicated averaging mechanism'.

From the way John described the sextant, it was clearly an ingenious and essential piece of kit, but not at all easy to use, and I wasn't surprised when he said that sometimes it felt that he was only able to navigate and find his way at all by the stars. How much easier it must have been when the sky was clear. John said that even though they did have good maps, often they simply did not know with any degree of accuracy where anywhere was and, 'sometimes', he told me with a twinkle in his eye, 'the instruction was to fly somewhere, with even the starting point not well mapped. Tricky! Not something we can appreciate today with so many ridiculously easy to use sat nav kits.'

Seated in front of the radio operator, John was one of the Lancaster's crew of seven. The bomb aimer sat at the front of the plane, in its nose, the pilot and flight engineer sat behind and just above him. Behind them were the navigator and radio operator and towards the middle and back of the plane were the mid-upper and rear gunners. Teamwork was paramount – each had a vital role to play to keep the others safe. They were all able to talk to each other through their communication kit, able to quickly alert each other to potential dangers. And in a Lancaster, John said, at least they could feel relatively safe, because of the altitude and speed at which she could fly.

With a wingspan of 102ft (31m) and equipped with four 1,280 horsepower Merlin engines, she was comparatively fast for a heavy bomber, but with a cruising speed of 180 knots could not outrun an enemy fighter. The crew relied on their well-trained gunners to alert them to enemy fighters and instruct the pilot to take the appropriate evasive action. 'Corkscrew port skipper – now!' might be the instruction that would initiate a series of violent manoeuvres until the attacker had either been shaken off, given up, or run out of ammunition.

But, even in the comparative safety of the Lancaster, the best performing of the RAF's heavy bomber fleet, there wasn't a single moment that John and the rest of the crew weren't aware of their vulnerability. The German 88mm flak guns were a continual menace. Earlier, while serving with 115 Squadron, John's aircraft had been severely damaged by a near miss from one of these which sent shrapnel through the fuselage just under the mid-upper gunner's seat – an inch or so higher and the gunner would have spent the rest of his days speaking with a much higher voice. Worse still, on that occasion, John said, the rudder had been partly shot away and it was only through well-practiced teamwork and the flying skill of the pilot that they were able to make it home to base using the throttles to steer instead of the rudders, which had become useless.

★★★

When I first met Flying Officer John Ottewell in the summer of 2017 at a gathering of RAF aircrew veterans, he was deep in conversation with Flight Engineer Dick Raymond, also a Lancaster crew member. They were discussing Operation Exodus, the return home of former RAF Prisoners of War (POWs) from Belgium to England. Dick had been a POW and John was one of a crew tasked with bringing the exhausted men home. They were trying to establish if they had met during this chaotic but somewhat celebratory repatriation period, in April 1945. Not surprisingly perhaps, given the passing of seventy-two years in between, they were unable to reach a definite conclusion. But, nonetheless, it was undoubtedly a conversation that they were delighted to be having.

Dick Raymond was one of hundreds of POWs who had not only spent weeks or months (or for some, almost all of the war) incarcerated in camps, but who had also been forced to endure the atrocious, now infamous 'Long March'. This was a 'march' that had begun almost five months prior to their eventual arrival in Belgium.

In the middle of a freezing night in mid-January 1945, German officers simply told their captives to leave the camps. They were instructed to head off into the silent cold of winter, pushed out because the Russian Army was on the move, westwards, towards them. The POWs were completely ill-equipped and unprepared for the horror of the march. For days they had to walk in temperatures well below zero, with very little to eat, becoming weaker by the day. Even though the German officers in charge of the marching prisoners must have been aware that the war was lost to them, they did nothing to ease the plight of the exhausted, hungry, cold captives – pushing them on as fast as they could, fearing the Russians behind. Perhaps, too, in making this walk 'home' as horrific as they could, they were exacting an act of revenge. The Germans knew they were defeated, so why not punish the Allies by inflicting suffering on this group of captive servicemen, already weak and vulnerable because of their time in captivity?

For some POWs it did prove to be a death march. Not all of them completed the journey. It was an agonising trek, described in more detail in Chapter 5 by Fred Hooker, a veteran with the courage to recall the painful memories for the sake of those who didn't make it, so their story is not forgotten. Dick Raymond – by virtue of his presence, of course – also came through the adversity the march threw at them and, together with Fred, eventually arrived in Brussels.

Operation Exodus began on 3 April 1945. It continued for around seven weeks, returning over 354,000 former prisoners to the United Kingdom via several receiving stations including Cosford in Shropshire, Dunsfold in Surrey and Wing in Buckinghamshire. It was an enormously complex operation, John told me, which had to be conducted as carefully as possible because so many of the prisoners were extremely weak and ill as a result of the conditions to which they had been subjected.

A number of different wartime bombers were used for the flights – Handley Page Halifaxes, Stirlings, even a B-17 Flying Fortress – but most of the POWs were brought home on the trusty Lancaster. It was on a Lancaster that John Ottewell accompanied some of the survivors home. He took them to Wing, 'We were able to squeeze 24 men into each flight,' he said. 'Not a very comfortable journey either, because they were quite squashed along either side of the fuselage with no proper seats'. I expect they didn't mind at this point. They knew they were going home.

In addition to their physical weakness, it was what many of the returnees chose to do with their chocolate that also stuck in John's mind. On arrival in the plane, each of the men was given a box with such goodies as cigarettes, biscuits and chocolate. Their hunger by this point might have been slightly eased with food in Brussels, but nevertheless chocolate would still have been a huge treat, a distant dream during the hardship of captivity. However, 'most of the men wouldn't eat it,' John said, 'they were saving it for their families back home.' Many of them, John told me, were of the understanding that swathes of the British population were also suffering from starvation and so they were more worried about their loved ones than themselves. It wasn't true, of course. There had been rationing, but the German officers accompanying them on the march had perpetuated this myth to further trouble the prisoners.

★★★

This, however, was not the only time during the Second World War that John Ottewell's service led him to help those suffering because of a lack of food. Starvation was a weapon that Germany inflicted upon thousands of the Dutch in the Netherlands – especially in the north and west. In the last year of the war, a German blockade cut off food and fuel shipments to farms and towns, resulting in a devastating famine known as '*Hongerwinter*' ('Hunger Winter') that led to the deaths of some 20,000 civilians (predominantly elderly men). Thousands more were affected and by the end of the war some 4.5 million Dutch were dangerously malnourished.

The Allies had been able to liberate parts of the south in the autumn of 1944, but the loss at the Battle of Arnhem in September of that year led to continued occupation in other areas. The failure of the Allies to secure a crossing over the Rhine during this battle marked a significant victory for Germany, who capitalised upon it with the infliction of the blockade. The conditions for the Dutch were also exacerbated by an unusually harsh winter which led to canals freezing over, thus cutting off further potential supplies.

Rotterdam, in the west, was an important industrial town whose people suffered terribly, not only during the famine but through-out the whole of the war – it was in May 1940 that it first fell into German hands. Hans Van Rij, now in his early eighties and living in Norfolk, was a war child who grew up here. Some of his earli-est memories are those of the devastation the war caused, but he also remembers with equal clarity the Allied operation to relieve the suffering of the famine, in the closing days of the Second World War.

'The *Hongerwinter* was awful,' Hans told me, recalling the many emaciated people he saw collapsing in the streets. He and his family struggled, but staved off starvation by eating lots of eggs provided by his grandparents, and blackbird pie, made from blackbirds caught in a trap his father made. 'The trap,' said Hans, 'was about 1.5m x 1.5m. When a bird came in, I pulled the rope and the bird was caught. Father did the rest, Mother did the cooking …' He went on to say, 'It wasn't particularly delicious, but these were desperate times. People would kill and eat whatever they could and try and grow whatever they could; I remember potatoes being planted in parks in the city, but,' he said, somewhat wistfully, 'it was rather hopeless. We were so hungry that tiny potatoes were eaten before they had a chance to get bigger.'

He remembered that after the initial bombing of Rotterdam he stood on a chair in his parents' kitchen, which enabled him to see the 'whole town' because the bombing left behind so much rubble. It was devastating – but, he said, 'Amazingly and probably because they were built so well, even after the bombing the library still stood, along with the church and the town hall.' However, his parents quickly concluded that central Rotterdam was too dangerous, too prone to repeated attacks for Hans to live with them there and he was sent to live with his grandparents in Zuid Holland (a province in the south that comprised a lot of small islands).

Hans' grandfather was a blacksmith and, even in the war years, managed to carve out a small income for himself and his family. However, even here there was no escaping the harm the Germans wanted to inflict and the destruction was achieved through flooding. The Germans deliberately flooded the islands with saltwater, not so much to cause drowning but to create chaos and devastation that ruined property and crops. Hans recalled dead hedges and trees everywhere and oilseed rape was about the only plant that grew well in the months that followed. The floods also made defensive flying very difficult because runways and airfields covered in water were invisible from the sky.

'The people living in villages near Rotterdam were slightly more fortunate, at least they could grow vegetables,' Hans said. 'But they were still hungry, and the legacy of the deprivation has – for many – never gone away.' Hans, for example, has lived with brittle bones throughout his whole life. 'It was just a horrible time,' he said. 'Horrible for everyone,' including – he was anxious to point out – the Germans, who, particularly in the closing weeks of the war, he knew simply wanted to go home. 'By the end of the war they had damaged our town enough. I think even they were sick and tired about the damage they caused,' he said.

However, it was when his father said to him at the end of April 1945, 'Tomorrow, Hans, you can watch the planes,' that he realised something was about to change. It was a strange thing for a young boy to hear (he was only 8 years old) when most of his childhood had been spent under German occupation and he had seen planes flying hundreds of times – mostly up high, of course, or too far away for him to take much notice.

The aeroplanes his father was referring to were very different. These were British and American bombers crewed by people like John Ottewell who were coming to the rescue of the hungry Dutch, in operations called Manna and Chowhound. These were extensive humanitarian operations during which food parcels were dropped from the aircraft. Operation Manna (named after the Bible story in the book of Exodus in which food miraculously appeared for the Israelites) was led by the RAF, assisted by squadrons from the Australian, Canadian and Polish air forces. Between 29 April and 7 May 1945 they dropped chocolate, biscuits and tinned food over the beleaguered towns during over 3,300 sorties.

Chowhound was the American operation – it began and ended a day later than Manna, delivering over 11,000 tonnes of nourishment. However, while both these operations alleviated much of the suffering, it still wasn't quite enough and a ground-based operation, Operation Faust, was launched on 2 May, bringing relief to the starving in the city of Rhenen, while it was still behind German lines.

All these operations were challenging, not least of all because the planes had to fly very low to deliver the parcels safely. Flying so low, of course, meant they were vulnerable to attack – after all, these were bombers that in 'normal' circumstances flew at heights of around 20,000ft (6,000m). For these operations, they had to fly lower than 500ft (150m). They were actually only able to do it in any form of safety after a truce was agreed with the German commander-in-chief that participating aircraft would not be fired upon within specified air corridors. But the dangers of flying at only 500ft were ever present.

Hans Van Rij spoke to me of the gratitude the people had for all the Allies who took part in these operations. 'Even in our weakness,' he said, 'we were aware of the risks men such as John Ottewell were taking for us.' He told me he will never forget seeing the planes flying so low, being clearly able to see the faces of the crew members on board. 'As soon as the parcels began to arrive, we knew this was the beginning of the end of the war. These tins – about 10" by 15" – were little miracles, each one gave us so much hope.'

John Ottewell supported the operation still as a navigator on Lancasters, but how different a mission it was for him – he was able to see the very people they were there to defend and care for – and of course the substance of what they were dropping was so completely different. His navigation skills for these flights were absolutely put to the test. They dropped their tins of supplies in double sacks, without parachutes, at the designated points:

It was difficult, and very important we were precise in those targets, because if we had deviated even slightly off course, we would have found ourselves sitting ducks, flying low and slowly over some of the most well defended areas in Europe. We wouldn't have lived to tell the tale.

But it only took a moment to look down and see the excruciating suffering of those who needed our help. The people were so thin, they were staring death in the face. Sometimes they were so desperate for the food parcels they would rush to the designated points, and we would run the risk of hitting them with the tins and sacks.

Some years later, John Ottewell returned to the Netherlands for a holiday. In a conversation with a Dutchman, he mentioned Operation Manna and was delighted when his new friend said, 'Yes I was there too, a child on the ground and very thankful for that food drop which saved my life!'

2

LAND OF HOPE AND GLORY – BILL CARTER

Bill was an engineer in the RAF. This is a story of the importance of music to Bill during the war, and of his work in the Middle East and Africa.

Victoria Panton Bacon with Bill Carter, at Duxford in June 2018. (John Smith)

Land of Hope and Glory, Mother of the Free, How shall we
extol thee, who are born of thee?
Wider still and wider shall thy bounds be set;
God, who made thee mighty, make thee mightier yet,
God, who made thee mighty, make thee mightier yet.
(Words: A.C. Benson, music by Edward Elgar, 1902)

Bill's was a musical war. As often as he could, he filled his loneli-
est wartime moments with uplifting tunes. Even in his darkest
times a melody would enter his head, strengthening him and
enabling him to lift the spirits of those around him. However,
it was the music he found in the most unexpected places that
makes Bill's musical wartime journey so fascinating and wonderful to hear about.

Music can bring light to even the deepest darkness. Notes can
tinkle away in our heads, and no one can take that away from us.
Bill Carter, 98 years old as this is written, cherishes his love of
music and many of the tunes that carried him through his Second
World War still resonate in his mind.

One of these is 'Land of Hope and Glory'. He told me of the
moment he, together with his comrades, were serenaded by a
middle-aged lady belting out Edward Elgar's famous tune as they
entered Cape Town harbour, in May 1942. To see her, and listen
to her contralto tones was a delight, he said, and the timing could
not have been better. It was truly comforting for all of them to be
reminded of England in that way – and much-needed comfort
it was.

The ship on which he was travelling, the *Dominion Monarch*, was
one of many in a large convoy of vessels transporting members of
all the services to India and the Middle East. Bill was on his way
to Iraq, via Cape Town, Durban and Bombay; a journey that had
started in the Firth of Clyde in Scotland. The convoy had taken
the men far into the Atlantic Ocean before heading south. When

they reached Africa, it brought to an end the first leg of their long journey, and this first leg had demonstrated to them just how cruel war could be.

All those taking part in war are vulnerable, be they aircrew in the sky, naval officers at sea, or infantry on land in tanks or on foot. Vulnerability was something they all had to simply get used to. In war, those who perish – not always, of course, but almost always – do so because they are unlucky. Bill witnessed such misfortune during this part of his journey.

Four ships in the convoy received direct hits from torpedoes, cruelly directed at them from U-boats. The *Dominion Monarch* could, of course, have been one of those struck, but it wasn't. Bill knew – as did his comrades – that it was only by the grace of God that he made it to Cape Town. The ships that were hit were some distance from Bill but afterwards he was clearly able to see the Allied cruisers and destroyers that approached the area of devastation to search for and attack the submarines.

There were hardly any survivors from the ships that went under. A successful, direct hit by a torpedo from a U-boat, striking the bottom of a ship, could sink it frighteningly quickly, drowning the targeted crew members, sometimes in a matter of minutes. On many occasions, before entering their watery grave, the unfortunate fellows would, ironically in freezing water, have been human fireballs, because one of the first things to happen to an exploding ship was for its oil to leak out. There would be gallons of oil on large ships, and much of it would cover those flailing around in the water, weighing them down, causing choking and impeding their ability to swim. They wouldn't stand a chance if they came close to fires caused by leaking oil and the breaking up of engines in the water.

After the war ended, Winston Churchill wrote, 'The only thing that ever really frightened me during the war was the U-boat peril.' Germany's best hope of victory lay in winning the Battle of the Atlantic. If Allied merchant ships had been successfully prevented from transporting food, materiel and troops between North America and Britain, the outcome of the Second World War could have been very different. Germany wasted no time in its attempt to win this oceanic war (known as the Second Battle of the Atlantic as Germany had waged a similar battle in 1917). On 3 September 1939, the very day Britain declared war on Germany, the British liner, *Athenia* was torpedoed by a U-boat, killing over 120 people.

However, as in the First World War, victory for Germany in the Atlantic was not to be, thanks in part to British intelligence which, as the war progressed, became sophisticated enough to track the whereabouts of threatening enemy U-boats. But, victory aside, Churchill's fear of the U-boat was not misplaced. By the end of the Second World War almost 3,000 Allied ships, including 175 warships, had been sunk by U-boat torpedoes. The Portsmouth Naval Memorial at Southsea commemorates the approximately 25,000 men who died at sea during both world wars – of these around 15,000 died during the Second World War.

So it was, on his arrival in Cape Town in the summer of 1942, that Bill Carter first realised how music could provide some calm in a way nothing else could. Nothing could fix the awfulness caused by the horror of the drownings, but the singing that greeted him and his comrades that day was a 'most welcome' distraction, he said, from their sadness, shock and general exhaustion. It was from here that Bill, a trained engineer, continued his wartime journey – a journey that had begun two and half years earlier when he signed up for service in the RAF.

After completing his training, he joined 5153 Squadron, a newly formed squadron that had been established to build and operate airfields in the Middle East. Before the war, airfields and almost all facilities of air force stations throughout the United Kingdom were designed, constructed and operated by the Civil Service, under the auspices of the Air Ministry Works Department (AMWD). However, when it became abundantly clear that airfields, power plants and capability had to be constructed in other parts of the world to support the overseas forces, 5153 Squadron was created to take on this task, because it was considered that creating such an important network of support shouldn't be the responsibility of civilians.

Bill was one of around forty early members of 5153 Squadron, comprising other qualified civil, mechanical and electrical engineers, in addition to plumbers, carpenters and car mechanics. All were initiated with an intense three-week training during which the importance of drilling in formation was drummed into them, as well as receiving instruction about the many different types of explosives and grenades they might come across in their wartime careers. Bill's basic training was in Warrington, after which he was posted to RAF Church Fenton in Yorkshire to hone his skills as an engineer, servicing and repairing the Rolls-Royce engines of the twin-engine Bristol Blenheim aircraft.

He then spent some months at Metropolitan Vickers, an electrical engineering company in Manchester, where he studied electric generating units, which were designed to be used with diesel engines. After a few months there, he was transferred to Ruston Hornsby in Lincolnshire to continue his training on diesel engines. During this time, the AMWD were fast developing plans to improve RAF airfields in the Middle East – an improvement programme that was seen as strategically vital in the bigger picture of the war effort.

Bill's training finally ended with a posting to RAF Grantham, where he worked closely with AMWD officials helping to plan the strategy for the urgent airfield improvements. Finally, in May 1942 he was ready for service, and the Second World War began officially for him with the long journey that commenced in the Firth of Clyde.

There was pride in Bill's eyes as he told me about 5153 Squadron's first posting, which was in the south of Iraq. Even though the terrain, 'basically an enormous burning hot desert', was totally alien to Bill and his comrades, the loss of the four ships in the early part of the voyage had taken its toll on their spirits and there was huge relief when they reached their destination. Cape Town had been their first stop and after resting there for a short while their route took them across the Indian Ocean to Bombay for a further rest and transfer to their last ship which headed into the Arabian Sea and along the Persian Gulf, to Basra.

5153 Squadron's first job was to install a diesel operating unit at the RAF base of Shaibah, in the south. Shaibah was one of two RAF stations then operating in Iraq – the other being Habbaniya, near Baghdad, further north. Both bases were created in the early 1920s, shortly after the end of the First World War and the establishment of Iraq as a country in its own right. In 1922, the United Kingdom signed a treaty with this very new country, protecting its interests, particularly in relation to oil. Iraq was essentially a sovereign nation, but in practical terms was administered by Britain, and the British oil industry was operating the rich oil fields of Iraq and the Persian Gulf. The treaty allowed for the unrestricted movement of British forces throughout the country, but in order for the UK to fulfil its purpose the smooth running of the two air bases was essential.

It took 5153 Squadron just over two months to build the diesel unit, following which RAF Shaibah was able to operate with far greater ease and effectiveness. 5153 wasn't alone at the base – they were with RAF colleagues of the resident 244 Squadron, as well as Czechoslovakian and Russian civil engineers who had been commissioned to work with them in the building of an additional electric generating plant, of which the diesel unit was to be a part. Bill spoke of how they all worked well together, respecting each other and enjoying each other's company – essential, not only in the completion of their tasks, but important because as well as working together, they slept and ate together and were billeted in cramped and compact quarters.

A benefit aside from job satisfaction, Bill told me, was the opportunity they had to learn each other's languages. He had no idea when he signed up to the RAF that he would end up learning how to say, 'Boy that is a fine piece of pipe' in both Czechoslovakian and Russian. There was a glint of naughtiness and delight in Bill's eyes as he told me this. Both the Czechs and the Russians, he said, were an extremely bright bunch of young men, most of whom, thankfully, also had a terrific sense of humour.

From the mugginess of Shaibah, Bill's next stop was the uninhabited desert island of Masirah, situated off the south-east coast of Saudi Arabia. On arrival, Bill said, he was not alone in experiencing overwhelming fear because of the gaping uncertainty about how they were going to manage. Aside from a beachhead with a small jetty, to which a 100-ton barge was tied for water transport, there was practically nothing.

5153 Squadron's task in Masirah was to build an aerodrome for 240 Squadron. This squadron was attached to Coastal Command, and its function was to defend the Persian Gulf, the Arabian Sea and parts of the Indian Ocean from submarine attacks on Allied supply routes.

However, before they could get on with their work they had, first, to build their accommodation. Initially, they slept on and under canvas draped from trees, but it wasn't too long before their sleeping quarters became slightly more sophisticated – they managed to create roughshod billets out of hundreds of empty 4-gallon petrol tins which they filled with sand to weigh them down. These cans contained fuel which had been supplied, mostly, by the nearby Kingdom of Oman for use by the crews flying Wellington bombers, carrying out patrol duties. Masirah proved to be a safe and relatively straightforward place for the crews to land, refuel and take off again to finish their patrol. The petrol cans were left behind, and it wasn't long, Bill said, before Masirah became affectionately known as 'Petrol Tin Island'.

Dormitories established, the real work began and, using the equipment brought to them on the various visiting ships, Bill and his comrades created roads and runways as best they could. Paraffin flares provided lighting and much time was spent levelling tracks, drilling wells and building a sanitation block.

Their food, Bill said, was mostly 'hard tack'. Turtle became a very important part of their diet – not only the animals themselves, but also their eggs. The creatures would come out of the water up to the beach, venture onto the land for about 100 yards and lay their eggs in clusters of around fifty in the sand hills. Each egg was around the size of a table tennis ball, but with soft skins that had to be gently pulled open to get to the food inside. Turtle eggs can't really be compared to a cooked chicken egg because apparently the white will always refuse to set – no matter how long it is cooked it remains viscous and runny – unpalatable, unless you were terribly hungry. Bill recalled a veritable turtle feast, however, one day on Petrol Tin Island when a mother turtle, huge – weighing over half a ton – was found on her way back to the sea and was hauled onto a truck and delivered to the squadron cook, a Cornish friend of Bill's called Jack Foss, who boiled her up and delighted the men accordingly.

They were not totally alone, however, and their diet was supplemented on occasion with extra food (bread, biscuits, potatoes, sugar, etc.) that arrived by ship from Karachi – deliveries that also included much-needed fresh water, as well as building supplies for the day-to-day work. There was welcome support, too, from Oman, which – in addition to supplying fuel for Coastal Command – produced generous supplies of nutrition and fresh water, as well as additional materials. Oman was one of the smallest of the seven Persian Gulf States and had declared war against

Germany in September 1939. It clearly welcomed the opportunity to support 5153 Squadron with their work.

Bill recalled that after 5153 Squadron had been on Masirah for about a month they were happily surprised by the sudden arrival of about fifty Omani labourers, who turned up on the island to help with them with their work. This proved very successful, enabling considerably speedier progress than there might otherwise have been. Bill said that the men were under the control of a senior Omani court official, who arranged for them to sleep in a temporary 'canvas village' and even though facilities on Masirah were extremely basic, the official managed to reside in 'considerable style', also hosting dinners to which Bill and his comrades were invited. These were 'splendid occasions,' Bill said, 'lots of different meats and fish, brought over from Oman.' At the first dinner they attended, Bill told me how they all ate too much – because it is an Omani custom to give a diner more food when their plate is empty – unless they indicate they are full by turning over their cup.

5153 Squadron was on Masirah for just over a year. After what Bill described as a challenging, exhausting but rewarding twelve months, he was finally transported out of Petrol Tin Island by air to Habbaniya, then by road through the Kirkat oilfields and along the route of an old pipeline to Israel, then to Egypt. By this time, Bill recalled, the long and difficult conflict in North Africa, Egypt and Libya had almost come to an end. British Field Marshals Alexander and Wavell had made strong advances against the Italians, but when the Germans joined in, General Rommel successfully pushed the Allies back, almost to Cairo. However, it was a fairly short-lived offensive on the part of the Germans because Field Marshal Montgomery came to the rescue, taking command of the Eighth Army. He stabilised the Allies' defences, built up supplies and manpower and launched the second famous El Alamein offensive, pushing the Italians and the Germans out of the region.

Beginning on 23 October 1942 and ending some three weeks later, this was strategically a hugely significant victory for the British, and 'Monty' led almost 200,000 British, Greek, Polish and French troops in over 1,000 tanks to victory in northern Egypt. The battle commenced with Operation Lightfoot, during which two channels were created in the minefields that the Allies were seeking to take, enabling them to progress their attacks. From this position, Monty commanded his troops to fight the Axis forces – 'crumbling' them as much as possible, was the phrase coined by Monty. It was a very difficult battle – the minefield 'corridors' were heavily congested, and the enemy fought hard with anti-tank guns – but Monty kept his nerve and seized victory some three weeks later, after the completion of Operation Supercharge, which was the code name for the final onslaught of attacks.

On 3 November, during the height of the battle, German Field Marshal Rommel said, 'The battle is going very heavily against us. We're being crushed by the enemy weight … we are facing very difficult days, perhaps the most difficult a man can undergo.' He was predicting the crushing defeat that was to come.

Victory, when it came, was an important morale boost for British generals and politicians, because it was the first (and only) land battle won by the British and Commonwealth forces without American support. Prime Minister Churchill said, 'Before Alamein we never had a victory. After Alamein we never had a defeat.'

General Rommel, however, was not yet defeated – the battle was a turning point for the Allies, but it did not bring about the end of the war in North Africa. Rommel's troops retreated almost immediately after Al Alamein to Tunisia, from where another, much longer battle took place. Beginning a couple of weeks after Alamein ended, it finally concluded with victory for the Allies in the middle of May 1943.

The Allied victory in May 1943 brought about the end of the Second World War in North Africa, so when Bill and his comrades arrived there around this time, 5153 Squadron had little proper work to do beyond repairing damaged aerodromes in parts of Egypt and Libya, where they were posted for the last two years of the war. They were, however, also given the additional duty of managing the prisoner-of-war camps, housing German and Italian POWs.

Bill told me he was thankful for the time they had on their hands. They were well looked after and spent much of their leisure time with the prisoners, playing sport and generally larking around. However, music also played a big part in their lives and it was while Bill was in North Africa that three things happened, which Bill told me he will never forget.

It was the piano that Bill enjoyed playing the most. I should just explain that the North African bases where they were staying were American, and the Americans equipped themselves very well with items to entertain as well as sustain. Bill said there was often a keyboard to be found, and his US comrades were only too pleased to share what they had with the British. As he and 5153 Squadron travelled around the area, repairing the aerodromes as they went – both in Egypt and Libya – they played their music whenever they had the chance, performing to the other troops.

They would often stay in transit camps, under canvas, which he said was wonderful as the nights were dark, the stars were bright, and the climate was kind. However, one morning he was horrified to wake up in his tent next to his friend, the drummer in his band, to discover he had been stabbed and robbed during the night. To this day, Bill does not understand how it was that he – and the others in the tent – did not wake during the murder, which they thought was almost certainly inflicted by a local Arab. Stunned, distressed and stricken by grief they reported the murder as soon as they could to the station commander, whose responsibility it was to deal with the body and carry out an enquiry.

Bill's next memory was a far happier one. While he was staying in a transit camp in Benghazi, he was thrilled by the arrival the famous American baritone singer Nelson Eddy, who visited them as part of a two-month tour, giving concerts for military personnel. Bill was excited, not only with the chance to meet him, but even more so because he found himself playing the keyboard for him because Eddy's right-hand man that evening was unwell. Together, they performed some of Eddy's most famous songs, including 'I'll see you again' and 'Rose Marie'.

His next recollection is another happy one, and explains why Giuseppe Verdi remains one of his favourite composers and his 'Requiem' one of his favourite pieces of music. Bill and his friends were taken completely by surprise one evening by some Italian POWs who they were looking after. Suddenly, the POWs burst into song, treating them to a performance of Verdi's 'Requiem', sung beautifully, said Bill, with harmonies in all the right places.

It was a mark of respect and gratitude, I am sure, to Bill and his friends for treating the POWs as kindly as they could. I expect Bill would have felt they had no reason not to be as gentle and generous because the war was all but over. I am sure that performing it was a wonderful experience for the prisoners themselves. In the words of Verdi:

> May light eternal shine upon them, O Lord, with Thy Saints for evermore: for Thou art gracious.
> Eternal rest give to them, O Lord, and let perpetual light shine upon them:
> With Thy Saints for evermore, for Thou art gracious.

3

PATIENT ENDURANCE
- PAT RORKE

Pat Rorke was living in Burma when it was bombed by the Japanese in 1941–42. This is the story of her upbringing there, and her exodus to India after Burma became too dangerous.

Patricia Rorke, Private. (Joss Sanglier)

YRUHQ S LDPXNGOKMIEBFZCWVJAT !!!

At first glance, the above mumbo jumbo seems like an incomprehensible chaos of gibberish (it is!). You may have just glanced through it and moved straight to this paragraph without giving it a second thought. Indeed, it is a good thing if you have; the untrained mind cannot easily make sense of such a random scramble of letters that contains no apparent sequence or order. If it could, we may not have won the Second World War, because during the war, the translation of pages and pages of 'gobbledygook' like this ultimately contributed to victory. Contained within letter combinations, such as the above, was intelligence that would be vital to Allied commanders across the country, and across the world. This intelligence informed, for example, the whereabouts and planned strategy of the enemy. It was crucial that it didn't fall into the wrong hands, so it was buried as carefully as it could be, often within letters thrown together to be decoded only by those for whom the message was intended.

The intelligence was contained in the millions of messages constructed in secret German military code, famously known as the Enigma code (although there were many variations), which were gathered predominantly from radio signals at Bletchley Park in Buckinghamshire throughout the war years. Once obtained, either through radio or other machines, the German code – cypher – was then decrypted by the brilliant minds at Bletchley using special equipment that turned the analysed information into intelligence reports, which were passed on to commanders who used the information to their advantage.

To prevent the enemy finding out that their cyphers had been successfully decoded, the Bletchley Park reports were often made to look as if they had come from spies working abroad and information was sneaked into jumbles of letters – usually to be decoded on machines that were rather like typewriters, although larger and with wheels attached, called Type-X machines. These were installed at outposts throughout the world, at intelligence-receiving offices known as Special Liaison Units (SLUs).

It was at one of these units in New Delhi, in India, that Pat Rorke – now 94 – worked for the last two years of the Second World War. A member of the Women's Auxiliary Corps, Pat started her work in the unit as a very junior officer working with other girls of her age, cataloguing hundreds and thousands of numbers and letters that were sent through to them from Bletchley. These were long lists that contained information to be decoded on a Type-X. The information was 'very, very hot', Pat said. 'It was mostly about the movement of Japanese aircraft carriers, but also sometimes about the ships that were part of their navy, which had been so horribly destructive.'

These important signals were gathered at three units in the Far East, which made up three points of a triangle – one was in Bangalore in southern India, one in Visakhapatnam in the Bay of Bengal (in the Indian Ocean) and the third was in Trincomalee, off the north-east coast of Ceylon (now Sri Lanka, after it was renamed in 1972 when it became a republic within the Commonwealth).

The staff located at each of the three points worked together, homing in on the call signs of Japanese aircraft and ships in the region, and when a signal was located it was quickly sent through to Bletchley to be decoded. It was then sent through to the SLU (concealed in hundreds of other letters and numbers) to be decoded again, and passed through secretly, up the chain of command. It was at this point that lives were potentially saved.

'It was extremely hard work,' Pat said, 'especially at the beginning.' With only a vague understanding of why she was doing what was asked of her, she worked with a small number of other young girls whose job it was to simply catalogue the thousands of digits that came through to their unit. 'We were all quite cross-eyed by the end of the day!' she said:

… but we worked hard because we knew that what we were doing was important and had a feeling if we did it well – which we could if we concentrated – we could save lives. Type-X was a really fantastic machine, absolutely marvellous. It would (simply!) take in the hundreds of meaningless digits (we put in it having received them from Bletchley) and out of it would come clear English. I know now that the Germans had unwittingly helped the codebreakers by giving (and explaining) their cypher codes to the Japanese. Little did they know they were being so rapidly deciphered by the clever team at Bletchley, who were sending anything relevant to us.

It was a fairly small unit: three Royal Air Force Type-X operators among a tight-knit team of around a dozen altogether, including the boss Bill Sanglier, who Pat married in Calcutta in February 1945. While they couldn't really talk to each other, they were busy falling in love! Pat was very fond of all of them. She looks back on those years as happy ones; bittersweet of course because it was wartime. The unit functioned day and night. Work was undertaken in shifts, but Pat and the other women were never asked to work at night.

Pat was promoted to the role of Sergeant in 1944, after which she left to train as an officer at the Officer Training Unit in the Himalayas. Following this, she returned to the Special Liaison Unit and only then was she told she was a member of 'Team Ultra', a status that she had previously not known about. (The intelligence gained as a result of decoding was known as 'Ultra'.)

Talking to Pat at her Buckinghamshire home, coincidentally not far from Bletchley Park, which is now a thriving museum, she told me how proud she is of having been a 'Bletchleyette' or 'Billy Filly', as the women who were part of this operation were known. By the end of the war, over 10,000 people had been part of this operation – also known as Britain's 'Ultra Secret' – of whom three-quarters were women. However, apart from those working in the high echelons of the intelligence business, for thirty years after the end of the war, the word 'Enigma' meant very little, a catchy word perhaps, but mysterious and little understood, because in spite of the scale of work undertaken and its recorded success, the secrecy enshrouding it continued. Even though Bletchley Park, also known as 'Station X', was the beating heart of intelligence gathering throughout the war, during those years its very existence was a closely guarded secret. It had an alias of being a radio factory, and even though it employed hundreds, the pretence was largely successful.

At the time, for the same obvious reasons of safety and security, Pat and the staff at her unit were strictly forbidden from discussing their work with anyone, even with each other. She said:

> Looking back, it is extraordinary that the secret of all this work was so well kept. But we all learnt how to keep quiet, together, about what we were doing. I think partly the war was so frightening it helped you keep quiet – we weren't even allowed to talk about it with the people we actually worked with. But actually we didn't want to discuss it, how awful it would have been to accidentally let something slip that caused terrible consequences. We were all in the same position; we all knew we were just small cogs in a huge wheel – doing something important but only doing it by force of circumstance. I didn't feel important, thankfully I suppose, none of us did. We just wanted the war to be over. I think if we had felt important, we would have started to talk. And that could have been fatal.

Pat reminded me of the phrase, 'loose lips sink ships'. She said that sometimes she and the other members of staff would relax and socialise together, and with people outside their unit, too. She said that while they were very careful not to discuss anything about the workings within the unit, discussions about the war in general were inevitable and quite often, she said, this led her to hear things that she knew were plainly wrong, but always, she said, 'even then, bursting to right a wrong, we had to keep quiet'. 'It used to drive me crazy!' she said:

> … and I would calm myself by thinking of Rudyard Kipling's poem 'If', for 'If I could keep my head when all about me are losing theirs …' I knew I would just about be able to keep my mouth closed.

To conquer the enemy, the Allies had to know what their game plan was. Breaking the code was therefore essential; but it was far from a given that it was possible. For years prior to the Second World War – including throughout the First World War and the intervening war years – attempts to gather information were made and partial successes were recorded. However, as the Second World War approached, British understanding of German cypher was far from sufficient. The intelligence divisions of the three services still had their own sections within what was then the government's intelligence service, GC & CS (Government Code and Cypher School). Pride and political divisions had to be put to one side, and when the Second World War was announced at 11 a.m. on 3 September 1939 by Prime Minister Neville Chamberlain, Bletchley Park was faced with a race against time to break the German codes.

Key battles and milestones were clearly won, eventually, as a result of the German Enigma cypher being successfully decoded, and on countless other occasions the use of the intelligence saved lives as it enabled us to be ahead of the enemy. For example, our crucial victory in the Battle of the Atlantic may not have been achieved without the amazing work of the code breakers and the risks undertaken by those whose role it was to gather the information.

The complexity of the whole operation was illustrated, for example, on 9 May 1941, when Royal Navy crew members on board the naval vessel *Bulldog* successfully captured the German submarine U-110 and seized an Enigma machine and code books that were found on board. This marked a key turning point in the war and the information that was discovered was put to use throughout the rest of the Battle of the Atlantic and in the Arctic. As the late British General Harold Alexander put it, 'The knowledge not only of the enemy's precise strength and disposition, but also how, when and where he intends to carry out his operations brought a new dimension to the prosecution of the war.'

One of Bletchley's many successful code breakers, the late Sir Harry Hinsley OBE, said he believed it was because of the Ultra intelligence gathered that German General Rommel failed in his campaign to occupy Egypt in 1942, and had he done so the reconquest of the whole of the North Africa region could have been set back, resulting in a change of the timetable for the invasion of France and even Operation Overlord (D-Day, June 1944) would probably have been delayed by up to two years.

Prime Minister Winston Churchill, shortly after the war, praised the code breakers, not only for their undoubted skills, but also for their respect for the secrecy of their work. He called the decrypts his 'golden eggs'. They had been laid, he said, by the 'geese who never cackled'. The 'eggs' referred to the messages that were successfully decoded on the Enigma machine and the 'geese' were the code breakers.

Pat Rorke joined the Women's Auxiliary Corps when she was almost 20 years old. India, however, was not her home – she had no choice but to travel there with her family as a refugee from Burma after it came under attack by the Japanese towards the end of 1941. The daughter of Michael Rorke, by trade a motor engineer but also a lay preacher within the Methodist Church, and Enid Wilkins, Pat was born and brought up in the Burmese capital, Rangoon. She didn't have a privileged upbringing, but a peaceful childhood, living with her siblings among children of different cultures and backgrounds, with a sense of belonging that was instinctive because both her parents had long had family ties with this part of the world.

Her mother, Marguerite Enid (known as Enid), was born in Malaya in 1896 (a year after it became a member of the British Empire), and her father's family, the Rorkes, also had long connections with this part of the world. Her paternal grandfather, John Rorke was a colour sergeant in the Bedfordshire Regiment and took part in the Third Burmese War, between 1885 and 1887. He married Ginny in 1885, herself an army child, whom he met in India.

Enid was one of eight children, but sadly three of her siblings died in infancy and, during the childbirth of her youngest brother, her mother died, leaving her father (Pat's grandfather) a widower tasked with the bringing up of five children. However, he too died not long afterwards, and Enid and her brothers and sisters were cared for by a close uncle and aunt.

Pat has written and also told me about the burden of sadness she knew her mother carried because of her parents dying so young. She wrote, 'We had to carry on … the sorrow had to be buried so the living could be served and cared for. Burying sorrow is still part of the pattern of human endurance.' Her mother's strength has been a guiding factor, said Pat, throughout her whole life, particularly during the war years as Burma fell to the Japanese.

After growing up as childhood friends, Enid and Michael married in Rangoon in 1920, shortly after Michael's return from England after serving for Britain in the First World War. Pat was born in Rangoon in October 1923, the second of three daughters, Eileen was born eighteen months earlier and her youngest sibling, Grace, was born in 1930. Her first brother, Alan, was born in 1928, a year after another sister was born but was sadly too weak to survive. Thomas arrived in 1929.

Pat looks back on the early years of her childhood with much fondness. Burma, then, was a peaceful country. However, her contentment was punctuated by times of difficulty – when she was just 4 years old her parents returned to England for a number of months, following a vicious blow to the head received by her father while working in his workshop. She and Eileen were left behind, cared for by their grandmother so her parents could travel to England and Michael could receive the medical care he urgently needed. At no point did the sisters ever think their parents wouldn't return to Burma, and indeed they did, with Michael much healed and both of them parents for a third time.

During our meeting, Pat spoke extensively about her upbringing in Burma, which she is so grateful to have had. She has written about it eloquently and beautifully in her book *Every Common Bush*. This chapter, in keeping with the theme of this book, is predominantly about her experience of the Second World War and much of it is dedicated to the fall of Burma, which had an impact upon the course of her life. However, her childhood was so rich and colourful that I feel compelled to just write a little about it. It was also from these formative years that she drew strength to cope with what the war threw at her.

For example, she has written in her book about some of the meals she remembers from her childhood. When she stayed with her maternal grandmother, she was allowed porridge in the morning with syrup. She wrote:

[of a] golden ribbon that slowly pleated itself into a steaming bowl of thick porridge, which was mesmerising; this was a small moment of the day that should never be hurried. The motif on the tins is the same today as it was then; a lion, a swarm of bees and the legend 'out of the strong came forth sweetness'.

Pat also, of course, wrote about curry, infinite varieties of which they usually had for lunch, blended together on a black stone slab with a rolling pin moulded out of the same stone. Each curry had a subtlety of taste that she has lost forever, she said wistfully, because never in this country has she been able – or found anyone else able – to replicate the delicacy of those flavours. One of her favourite curries comprised dry beef, served with pepper water made from tamarind and another was chicken mulligatawny, 'swimming in lovely yellow gravy, eaten with fragrant rice, crunchy poppadoms and slices of lime'.

Much about the natural world was a source of fascination and joy for Pat. In her book, she wrote about:

> … the birds, the ones like crows and mynah birds that were so common we barely noticed them, and the exotic bottlebirds that hung their woven nests in the Palymyra palms that grew in the garden, and the kites, too, that circled above the trees.

During our conversation, she also fondly recalled time spent with her sister Eileen, simply 'sharing each other's thoughts'. She wrote:

> There was a corner of one of the verandas overlooking the lane where we could sit on the floor with our backs against the wooden wall of the house, just talking. Life was full of wonder, there was so much to think about and dream about.

However, the warmth that was so much part of her life wasn't a protective blanket all of the time. Her family suffered hardships too, including severe financial difficulty at one stage of her upbringing which threatened their livelihood. Neither were the family sheltered from the challenges of life beyond their own world, such as natural disasters including the earthquakes and tremors which made them all feel so vulnerable.

She wrote of an earthquake she experienced at the age of just 6½. Pat felt the movement of a large tremor, which centred in Rangoon, not far from their home. Hundreds of people suffered the full impact of the earthquake, with many dying and others losing their homes. She wrote of how, in the home they were in:

> … a tray of glasses slid off the table and crashed to the floor. We all clung to anything that seemed to promise stability. The long chains of beads that formed a curtain that separated the sitting room from the dining room swung and twisted like snakes, and the piano set up an eerie humming. I was only six and half at the time; these are the limits to my memories of the quake, but those are vivid.

It was around the same time, in the early 1930s, that Pat first saw how cruel mankind could be. Rangoon became engulfed in the horror of racial riots that suddenly erupted between the Bengali Indians and the Burmese. These were violent and offensive riots that left many dead, mostly Indians, with whom the Burmese had run out of patience. Pat wrote:

> There were so many Indians living and working in Rangoon that one could be forgiven for thinking it might be a city in India. Add to that the number of other 'foreigners', among them Chinese, British and other Europeans. No wonder the Burmese felt outnumbered in the capital of their own country.

Her father did all he could to help the injured and comfort the bereaved. He was able to do so because he was neither Burmese or Indian, and he was driven to do so because he was a devout Methodist. It was a frightening, unpredictable episode of her childhood, which left Pat and her family 'marooned' in the way that warfare does. The riots eventually calmed, but left with them 'a sober aftermath', she wrote:

What could I really comprehend at the tender age of six, rising seven? The real world, with its political undercurrents, the struggle to be free, the struggle to rule wisely when ruling itself was under attack, the constant dilemma of authority caught between maintaining itself or abandoning the responsibilities it had created with the risk of ensuing chaos, the never ending errors of judgement, the cruelties of man to fellow man, these things passed me by most of the time; only when they impacted on the small happy world that my parents tried to make for their children, did I begin to comprehend, but slowly.

By painting a picture of the family she grew up in and the environment around her, I hope it will help you appreciate Pat's deep sadness when the country changed so much and she was forced to leave, as Burma began to fall to the Japanese. Pat was just 18 years old when the first bombs landed on her precious land – two days before Christmas in 1941.

It was the beginning, Pat wrote, of 'the past being destroyed; the future looming as impenetrable as an ocean must be to a submarine whose instruments have all failed'. She learnt, during the awfulness of seeing Burma weakened at the hands of the Japanese, to 'put a lid on regret, disappointment, longing, anticipation – in fact any emotion at all that would weaken my ability to cope'.

In 1940, with the Second World War well underway, Pat and Eileen had begun undergraduate studies at Rangoon University; Pat was studying maths. However, the heightened political tensions that were being felt throughout the country because of the war were also being felt deeply among the students at the university, and this created difficulties for Pat. Burma was, at this time, still under British rule, but this did not mean that all of the Burmese were on the side of the Allies; a good number were not, she said, and some students left to go to Tokyo, to take up their studies there. She described the Students Union as a 'hotbed of activists who wanted to wrest Burma back from the British'. She knew they had every right to feel as they did, and to an extent she said she felt she was under suspicion because of her British nationality.

For weeks before the incursions began, the impending future disturbance of war was being felt in many parts of Burma, including along the Burma Road, which was a lifeline for China as it was the route used by the Americans to deliver vital aid and armaments to its ally. China and Japan had been at war since the mid 1930s, and by the start of the Second World War, Japan had successfully taken most of China's ports – help from the USA was much needed.

During the early part of the war, the Japanese realised they could inflict considerable harm on the Chinese by restricting their help from the USA, and began a concerted campaign to attack trucks delivering aid from the air – flying from Japan and making their way to Chungking, the wartime capital of China. Because the road ran through parts of Burma, in the mountainous region to the east of Burma and the west of China, the attacks along this road put the war that was raging in China firmly on Burma's doorstep.

In the capital Rangoon, much was being done to prepare the people for the likely precarious days ahead. Pat told me of enforced blackouts and air-raid practices – she recalled how her friends who were still at school were instructed by their teachers to stick crisscrossed strips of paper on window panes in order to make them shatterproof and she remembered the loud cries of air-raid wardens who would run around in the town excitedly shouting out, '*Butti bund karo*! [Put out the lights!]'

The Japanese onslaught on Burma and in the Pacific region began in earnest on 10 December 1941, with the sinking – following torpedo attacks – of two British battleships, the *Prince of Wales* and the *Repulse*, resulting in the deaths of 840 Allies. The tragedies were inflicted within three days of the Japanese bombing of Pearl Harbor in Hawaii. From that moment, there could be no doubting the seriousness of the Japanese threat; their military strength and determination to dominate was real.

Pat was at university when she heard the news of Pearl Harbor and thus came to the realisation that her precious homeland was now a key target for occupation by the Japanese. Almost immediately, the cruelty of war was laid bare, with the Japanese students at the university being gathered together and ordered to leave. One of the students, Lillian, was a close friend of Pat's. 'That dear Lillian was now an enemy,' Pat said, 'was ludicrous. All I could do was watch, dumbfounded, as she was driven away.' The university closed, and Pat and Eileen returned to be with their family.

On 19 December 1941, the Rorke family left Rangoon for the last time, beginning their long journey to India. They did not leave a moment too soon as on 23 December the attacks on the capital began. Not content with simply dropping bombs, the Japanese flew low over the town, gunning down civilians in the streets, even targeting those sheltering in hastily dug trenches. This fatal raid was followed by another on Christmas Day. In all, around 2,500 people were killed on these two days alone and the same number again were injured. The disintegration of Burma had begun.

Early in January 1942, the Japanese focused their attacks on the coast and by the middle of the month the key coastal towns of Tavoy and Moulmein fell to the enemy. By 8 March, Rangoon itself was occupied.

Pat and her family were among thousands who were forced to leave the country because of the painful events that were unfolding. The Rorkes' first staging post en route to India was Maymyo, a hill station in the northern Shan states of Burma, where they stayed for a number of weeks with other refugees at a hostel. Pat's younger siblings fortunately found a teacher among its residents who passed the time at the hostel quite productively with them. Eileen became a nurse and Pat busied herself as much as she could by helping with anything that was needed – including washing, cooking and childcare.

It was while in Maymyo that the reality of what was happening to Burma truly struck home – the country would never again be the same. They were there when Rangoon fell to the Japanese, and following the capture the Japanese began to advance northwards. Pat and her family had no option but, together with thousands of others, to continue their journey towards India. She said:

All around were the widening gaps in a society falling apart at the seams. There was a stunned pause after the air raids on Rangoon while the inhabitants of Burma came face to face with the ghastly suspicion that their country was actually about to be overrun by the Japanese. Many of the Indians began to flee. The Japanese battle cry 'Asians for the Asians', seemed to have been received with cynicism. What the Chinese, of whom there were large numbers in Burma, did particularly in Rangoon I have no idea, but they are a resourceful people and would have removed themselves from the path of the enemy. The British families whose whole purpose for being in Burma had ceased to exist moved to India. With servants leaving, households became disorganised. The average Burmese sat back and observed. They were divided amongst themselves. There were those who saw self-determination the British way, a process already in hand with the 1937 severance from the British government in India, and those who saw the Japanese coming as a means to an end. There were the vast majority who had little say in the matter and who had never had a say, even in the time of the Burmese kings, and who waited with Buddhist resignation for what destiny had ordained for them, whatever it may be.

On 17 March 1942, Pat left the Maymyo hostel to begin the next stage of her journey. Her departure, however, was only with her three youngest siblings and grandmother. Her mother, father and Eileen chose to remain in Burma. Her father had chosen to stay there to help the weary and injured, her mother knew she needed to be with him, and Eileen remained to continue her work as a nurse.

Pat wrote of the prayers they said before leaving, the last prayers they were to share together, ever, as a complete family. Their departure was late at night. Journeys had to be undertaken in this way so as to make them as inconspicuous as possible. She wrote of the crowded train they then boarded at midnight:

> … as sheep, with a shepherd who called us by name. As we were identified, he ticked us off on the list held in his hand, we were detached from the silent mass around him, and ushered to the third class carriages that comprised the entire train. No room for class divisions on this train: no comfortable padded bunks, no individual toilet facilities, no fans to cool the air; just hard slatted wooden seats, and a small room with a hole in-the-floor continental convenience.

The train took them to their next stop, an evacuee camp in Shwebo, via Mandalay and Sagaing, close to the enormous Irrawaddy River. The Irrawaddy, Pat wrote:

> [is] a long river, rising in the high mountain range in the north of Burma, which plunges and foams turbulently southwards through a series of spectacular defiles, then, tamed by the level floor of the central plains, meanders peacefully on its way, taking in the line of least resistance, till it fans out into a vast delta, where Rangoon is situated, through which its divided waters at last reach the Bay of Bengal.

The camp was a staging post for them; they were there for just under a week before transferring by plane. Shwebo was very basic, Pat said, crowded with a range of nationalities for whom Burma had become home, including Anglo-Burmese, Anglo-Indian, French, German, Greek, Italian and Portuguese. Pat said it was:

> [a] miracle of organisation. The unpaid, too often unsung, volunteers were there as usual, serving meals to the long queues, postponing to the last minute their own chance to be evacuated. Meals had to be eaten in shifts and those who spooned out baked beans, tinned bacon, stew, mashed potatoes and whatever else was on order must have been so tired. I do not suppose they were all native to the heat, the mud floors, nor even to servitude; but they filled the succession of proffered tin plates with good humour and helped speed us on our way. I enjoyed the sense of fellow feeling engendered by the communal life; everyone was friendly and interesting, and the levelling of society was good. For a while, who you were, where you came from, what your lifestyle was, had no consequence; we were all one.

It was from Shwebo that Pat left Burma for almost the last time (she has only returned once, briefly, in 1983). This visit was memorable and delightful because of the welcome she was afforded by immigration staff at the airport in Rangoon, who were thrilled to discover from her passport that she was born in Burma. Much excitement followed as she shared stories of her childhood with them.

With more anticipation than excitement, Pat's migration from Burma – with her young siblings and elderly grandmother – finally began. They were flown out of the country in a Dakota transport plane, landing some 230 miles away in Chittagong in neighbouring Bangladesh, an arrival that came as something of a relief as it was a bumpy, cold, uncomfortable journey. However, at least they felt safe. Upon landing on foreign soil for the first time, Pat could only wistfully think of her beloved homeland, despairing for the many remaining who had been unable to escape, many of whom were unable to defend themselves.

The war was, for Pat, the same as for thousands and thousands of people all around the world. It was a frightening and unpredictable episode of history that was dividing and separating loved ones and families, leaving thousands bereaved, causing injury and torture, and resulting in thousands more languishing as captives in prison.

Pat had no idea at this time when, or if, she would see her parents and Eileen ever again. She did see them, eventually, but on her eventual arrival in India they were far away, out of reach and out of contact, and she had to cope with the momentous circumstances of being responsible for her young family and grandmother in a new country, managing the anxiety which was an inevitable consequence of the uncertainty of her new world. Scant comfort at this stage was really only gained from knowing that she was far from alone in her predicament; indeed, those all around her were also sharing her lonely emotional struggle.

Travel, by this time, had to be seen as an adventure. Each leg of the journey was different, providing at least the opportunity to see dramatically beautiful parts of the new countries they were visiting. They left Chittagong on another night train that took them to Chandpur – still in Assam – from where they boarded a large ferry that steamed up the Padma River, towards Goalanda. From there, they disembarked the steamer to take another train to Calcutta.

The Padma River, Pat wrote, was 'so wide in parts that the banks of the river disappeared from sight, it was hard to believe we were not in the open ocean'. She wrote of the breakfast they ate while on board, and how they 'leant over the railings, watching the muddy waters of the river swirl on their way, marvelling at the immensity of this part of India, forgetting for a while that we were homeless'.

Finally she arrived in India, in Calcutta, in the east of the country. From this bustling 'cultural gem' of a city Pat and her small troop travelled by train for a further two days, eventually reaching Mussoorie, a hill town in the Dehradun region of the Himalayas, from where she would make her next emotional departure. This was 'a lovely spot,' she said, 'with a southern view over the plains from which we had come, and a northern view towards the everlasting snows.' Here they were accommodated in a unit within army family headquarters that were no longer being used.

Pat's first job was to find boarding schools for her siblings, which she did. Once they were settled, Pat had no option but to move on herself because the army accommodation was temporary and financially it would have been too hard for her to make a life for herself in Mussoorie. Fortunately, Pat and her grandmother were no longer alone; they had discovered they had cousins also living in the Dehradun district. Their home welcomed Pat and her grandmother, a home which Pat – in spite of missing her immediate family – revelled in, comforted by the warmth of her, albeit distant, relations.

Money, however, was short and soon after settling into this home she joined the Auxiliary Nursing Service at the Combined Indian Military Hospital in the town of Dehradun. Together with other young, inexperienced women, Pat was thrown into the deep end of the nursing world, caring for the steady flow of those who had been wounded on the border of India and Burma. The girls were kept busy all day long administering medicine, delivering and emptying bedpans, cleaning and dressing wounds – very importantly, each time checking carefully for any signs of deterioration in the healing process, in case of gangrene. They were trained, too, about malaria and pneumonia, spending time on wards dedicated especially to those suffering with such conditions. The suffering was made much worse by the soaring temperatures from which there was little escape.

Regarding her nursing career, Pat wrote of 'patients so badly injured or burnt it hurt one to move them'. She said she 'lived in a constant state of silent apology' and:

> ... soon learnt to respect, especially, the Indian soldier. Indian implied either Hindu or Moslem in the days before the separation of the subcontinent. I had grown up among the ordinary labouring Indians, the coolies, the servants, the shopkeepers, tram drivers, pullers of rickshaws, the drivers of *gharis*, itinerant tradesmen; but never the Indian soldier. They were remarkable. They were often in so much pain. But they were uncomplaining, long suffering and retained a sense of humour.

Pat worked hard by day and was cared for kindly and gently by her relations at home. However, she worried for her young siblings at their schools but could not easily make the journey to see them. Also, during this time she had no contact with her parents. She wrote, 'the silence between us and those still left in Burma was impenetrable, even my imagination could find no answers.'

Events in Burma were accelerating towards the last days of the invasion. April was the critical month of 1942. The Japanese advance northwards could not be halted, and Mandalay was seized on 30 April. Lashio, in the northern Shan states had already been taken by this date and the northerly town of Myitkyina, the location of the only airfield still in British hands, was captured at the end of May, marking the completion of the fall of the country.

There followed a mass departure of refugees from Burma. Thousands of natives and other nationalities were forced to leave as hastily as possible, beginning their long journey across the mountains in a state of chaos, fear and trepidation. For many, the journey was too hard, and they did not reach their destination. One of those who did not was a close uncle of Pat's – Tom, her father's brother. She wrote:

The full story of that terrible exodus will never be told. A thousand pitiful truths lie buried in the jungles between Burma and India. The roll can never be fully called. The survivors may in time have relived their ordeal for others, and perhaps purged the horror of it in the telling; but who can speak for the dead? Who can speak for Uncle Tom?

In telling me about it, Pat has spoken for them all.

Michael, Pat's father, occupied himself during this time looking after the hungry, sick refugees – a role which exhausted him, but he was focused and driven to do all he could to help. 'Fear makes ordinary people lose their heads,' Pat wrote:

[my father said] there were some who did, for there was much to fear. He told me they were living on the edge of chaos, but in the end some sort of sanity prevailed, and by the time the whole of Burma had fallen to the Japanese, everyone who could be had been evacuated by plane. The rest either walked or decided to stay behind.

Enid, Pat's mother, and Eileen had taken a plane while Michael Rorke chose to walk. He was among hundreds who bravely undertook the 600-mile journey from Myitkyina to India; a journey so exhausting that, Pat wrote:

… it left him gaunt, bearded, sick and like an old man, with shoes tied to his feet which were so sore he could barely stand on them.

At first the jungles and mountains were dry under foot, and the tracks were in good condition, but a monsoon broke in fury, rending their conditions a nightmare. The rain, mud, difficult terrain, streams that became raging torrents, the cold and lack of food took its toll. Daddy saw people drowning, dying from falls and suffering with malaria and dysentery. Some fell asleep and did not wake up. Daddy eventually arrived with nothing, discarding all his belongings because anything to carry was too heavy, he was so weak. During the journey he badly injured his back, but somehow kept going, putting one foot in front of the other.

After the war, you have to learn to live together, remember that you are all human … behind all these bare recounted facts lies a great tragedy that can be imagined but not relived by anyone who did not walk out of Burma by the Northern Route. Daddy saw too many people die in pitiful conditions, and Mummy – when they were reunited – said that despite his outward appearance of coping by day, he twitched and muttered in his sleep for months.

This is what war does. It litters our past, clutters the present and makes filthy the times that lie ahead. War changes people's bodies and minds; some are strengthened simply by their very survival, but far more are weakened, physically or mentally, hurt so badly that the dark cloud above them cannot be dispelled. For millions who suffer through war, restful sleep is a dim and distant dream.

Pat and the rest of the Rorke family lived through the downfall of Burma in the Second World War. Witnessing the collapse of a beloved land was a horror experienced by millions, in hundreds of different countries, cities and towns. Millions of families were torn apart as a result of enforced occupations. Millions of displaced people never returned home and were forced to make new lives.

The record of Michael Rorke's journey is important. His experience was appalling, but sadly far from unique. Long, tortuous journeys such as this were undertaken by millions of people who faced the agonies of knowing very little of their destination.

Pat and her family's experiences were perhaps fairly typical. In spite of the enormous challenges they faced, they did make the journey from their homeland to a new country and, while it was far from easy and they all had emotional barriers to overcome, they did settle and make India their new home, even if only for a relatively short time. The loss, though, of one family member – Tom – in all of this was tragic and painful, but families who did not lose someone were unusually fortunate.

Eventually, Pat was reunited with her parents. Firstly her mother, who she met in Kirkee (now Khadki), a small town in the north-west. Upon meeting her again, Pat wrote, 'Tears are not only for grieving, they serve very well for moments of great joy. There were many tears.'

Some weeks later, she saw her father again, too. Their reunion was in Bombay, where her parents had rented a flat and Michael had taken up a position in the RAF. Remarkably, he had recovered well after the trials of his long walk, and Pat commented on how handsome and vibrant he looked in his uniform. Pat's stay in Bombay with both of her parents was brief, but as happy as could be. That is another consequence of war; the pain and separation results in untold suffering – however, with deep lows often follow the headiest highs. The lows teach appreciation in a way that nothing else can.

Pat had, by the time of her visit to Bombay, already made the decision to leave nursing, instead choosing to enrol in the Women's Auxiliary Corps. The enrolment led her to the Special Liaison Unit, and the vital work she did to oppose the enemy that had so hurt her beloved Burma.

However, after the end of the war and shortly before leaving the Far East for good – and beginning her life with Bill in England – Pat was tasked with one more duty. Working in a military hospital, her job was to list the names of dead and wounded British servicemen, taking their names from identity cards sent to her by staff from other hospitals. She said that often the cards 'would be encrusted in blood, partially concealing the handsome face of a young man, men full of hope and determination'. She had to list the names, then destroy the cards:

> It was as though I was mourning for the families. I would see their faces as I slept at night.
>
> My job in the liaison unit was exciting, it was rewarding to know I was doing something for the war effort. But it wasn't until after the war ended, and I was handling the identity cards of these men, men who had all suffered so much pain that I began to truly understand the horror of war. It was so hard, but I wouldn't have done anything else.

Nine months later, after Pat travelled to England, so did the rest of her family. None ever returned to India. 'There began,' said Pat, 'our ordinary lives.'

However, Pat carries with her cherished memories of her childhood, never forgetting the fragrance of the food, the noise of the monsoons, the beauty of the Palmyra palms and the warmth of the people. Strengthened by her faith and the enduring love of her parents (even after they died), she keeps with her every day a card with some words of Mother Theresa written on it:

> Let nothing disturb thee, nothing affright thee; all things are passing, God never changeth. Patient endurance attaineth to all things; alone God sufficeth.

To end this chapter, Pat has given me one of the many poems she has written. This is one of her favourites; it is an Easter poem:

> What shall I say when I leave the garden?
> What shall I say of the empty tomb?
> 'Tell them he rose!'
> He is not here. Death was not His destiny,

Nor the silenced word. This place
Was but a quiet pause between His sacrifice
And the endless incredible out-pouring of His grace.
'Tell them He lives!'
Accept the miracle. Friday's pain and yesterday's
Long grey hours are gone. Out where
Men live, along the road, or in some quiet room, His spirit
moves – a living flame.
Go seek Him there!

4

AFT THE POOP DECK – DOUGLAS HUKE

Douglas Huke served in the Merchant Navy for the whole of the war, as a wine and bathroom steward. This story gives magnitude to the thousands of sea miles he travelled, including to Australia – twice.

Douggie Huke, taken on Douggie's 103rd birthday in July 2019. (Dan Millar)

On 24 July 1916, an unusual parcel was delivered at the Bramfield village post office near Halesworth, in Suffolk. The parcel was the gift of a son, Douglas Albert Jack, to Albert and Harriet Huke. At the time of his son's birth, halfway through the Great War, Albert was away serving with the Royal Horse Artillery.

Douglas was named after Field Marshal Earl Douglas Haig, as well as his father and maternal grandfather, Jack Farman. Earl Haig was then Commander-in-Chief of the British Expeditionary Forces on the Western Front, leading troops through some of the most difficult battles of the First World War, including the Battle of the Somme, which started a couple of weeks before Douglas was born. The atrocity of this battle lasted for four months, after which Haig ordered his (remaining) troops to retreat. Victory on either side could not be claimed, and thousands of lives were lost.

Field Marshal Haig has drawn criticism over the years for his failure to seize victory at the Somme, and it has also been written that what happened during those terrible months in 1916 probably helped to pave the way to victory two years later, not least because it allowed the Allies to recapture some strategic territory. Douglas thinks his father played his part in this battle, and has long been proud to be named Douglas, after Earl Haig, as well as his father.

At this point, Alfred Huke must also be remembered. Alfred was one of Albert's older brothers. Sadly, he did not come home. He was 39 years old when he died on a battlefield in France and is buried at the Vis-en-Artois Memorial, near Pas-de-Calais.

However, thankfully, Albert did come home. After the war ended, he took over his father's printing company, which was based in his home town of Lowestoft. While her husband was away, Harriet had moved 'inland' to Bramfield and was taken in by the owner of the post office because the shelling at home was too dangerous, especially for someone expecting a baby. After they were reunited, they settled again in Lowestoft and began their lives as parents together. Three years after the war ended, Douglas was delighted to become an elder brother to Marjorie.

However, these were difficult times. The First World War, in spite of the victorious outcome, had left behind a painful economic legacy that was felt not only in cities but also in rural communities up and down the country. Prior to 1914, Britain had been an economic superpower, but the war changed all of that. Financing the war itself cost billions of pounds and British trade with foreign nations that had flourished before the war all but dried up between 1914 and 1918, with countries who had purchased our goods finding alternative suppliers. By the early 1920s, Britain had slipped into the deepest recession in its history. Douglas recalled that many buildings in Lowestoft that had been badly damaged were not rebuilt, and he remembered the sadness felt by his father on having to lay off employees.

Few towns in Britain felt the legacy of the war more keenly than Lowestoft. In addition to its sliding economy, its geographical position as Britain's most easterly town had made it vulnerable to attack. Its own harbour was home to an important naval base, too, housing a fleet of armed trawlers that had been used to combat German U-boats. It was a busy harbour throughout all of the war, but it was on 25 April 1916, two months before Douglas was born, that this small town felt the pain of the war more than ever.

This was the day of what became known as the 'Lowestoft Raid', which saw vessels from the German High Seas Fleet bombard Lowestoft and nearby Great Yarmouth. It happened because of the Irish Easter Uprising, which had begun the previous day – this was an attack on British rule in Ireland by Republicans hoping for an independent Irish republic. Lowestoft was pulled into the conflict because about two years before the Irish rebels had sought support from other nations, including Germany – who had agreed to support them. It was during the High Seas Fleet's journey to Ireland, via the east coast, that Lowestoft was attacked. However, the German fleet was intercepted by vessels from the Harwich Striking Force Squadron of the Royal Navy. They failed to sink many of the enemy, but the result was that most of the enemy vessels returned to Germany, instead of progressing to Ireland. Twenty-one members of the Royal Navy were killed, in addition to three civilians, and nineteen local people were badly wounded.

So, even though peace was declared on 11 November 1918, when Douglas was 2 years old, as he grew up, he felt the impact of the First World War every day. There was no escaping the damage it had inflicted on his town, or the pain of grief suffered by so many. It was an environment in which, I expect, Douglas felt he had to grow up fast, and by the age of only 14, he, like many of his contemporaries, left school and entered the world of work.

Douglas left school in 1930. Times were hard, but people were doing their absolute best to make good lives for themselves – and something that was on an upward trajectory was the motor car. Douglas was fascinated and intrigued by the development of cars which, much to his father's disappointment, he found infinitely more fascinating than his father's printing equipment. Among other items, his father produced posters for Lowestoft Town Football Club, council minutes and flour bags for local bakers – nothing that excited young Douglas enough to follow in his footsteps.

Reluctantly, perhaps, Albert Huke let his son follow his heart. Douglas knows to this day how fortunate he was because, not long after leaving school, he found a job in a vehicle repair shop in Lowestoft, taking up a role that paid him 5s a week for fifty-one hours' labour. He worked there for two years, after which he took on a position in a wire and cable manufacturing company, where he worked on condensers for Ford T25 motor cars.

Douglas was lucky to find work, even though he worked extremely hard for relatively little. However, as the 1930s progressed, against a backdrop of a struggling economy and collective grief, people were also living with the impending fear of the next world war.

★★★

Amazingly, in spite of his 102 years, it was these pre-war years that Douglas spoke of first during the interview he had been so kind to grant me. He recalled the now-famous words of Neville Chamberlain, who said in September 1938 when he was prime minister, 'Peace for our time', during a speech that followed the signing of the Munich Agreement. This was an agreement signed by Hitler and Chamberlain, as well as the leaders of France and Italy, that allowed for the possible aversion of the Second World War, because it resulted in Germany being given hundreds of square miles of western Czechoslovakia, on the condition it did not attempt to occupy anywhere else at all.

It was six months after Chamberlain made this speech that 22-year-old Douglas Huke embarked upon his maiden voyage as a member of the Merchant Navy. This journey, momentous for young Douglas, began on 21 April 1939.

On board the SS *Oronsay*, a 20,000-tonne steam ship, he departed Tilbury Docks, setting sail for Fiji in the Pacific Ocean, some 10,000 miles away. He was employed as a steward in the ship's kitchen, responsible for cleaning plates and crockery for the passengers in the lower decks.

Douglas didn't know what to expect and didn't really know what was expected of him either. But, he said, 'The money was good, I wanted to save. So I signed on.' He did not even know where he was headed until the ship set sail. 'That was all part of the secrecy, waiting to find out where we were heading.'

He said:

Something I remember quite clearly about this first journey happened as we left England. We were sailing along the Thames and going into the Channel, and I saw an aircraft trailing a notice with Chamberlain's same words 'Peace in England for our Time'.

Douglas told me he remembered thinking at that point it was 'too late for that message. There was no peace, it felt as though war had already started.'

While Douglas was at sea on his maiden voyage, preparations at home for the Second World War were well under way. In addition to the expected bombing raids, it was feared that poison gas might be deployed as a weapon of war, and gas masks in their thousands were being manufactured. An Air Wardens Service was also established, run by volunteers who took on duties including investigating reported unexploded bombs, administering first aid, and keeping people calm during practice, and real, air raids.

'Blackout' trials began in many cities at the beginning of 1939, and the day war was announced the government passed a bill called the National Service (Armed Forces) Act, which imposed conscription on all men between the ages of 18 and 41, obliging them to register for service. Only those who were deemed medically unfit were exempt, as well as those working in 'reserved occupations' such as baking, farming, medicine and engineering.

And, of course, as it turned out, these preparations were absolutely necessary. The 'peace' Chamberlain had negotiated in Munich in September 1938 did not prevail. Even then, it was a fragile peace that I expect Chamberlain could only hope against hope would last. But it did not.

On 3 September 1939 at 11 a.m., Prime Minister Chamberlain announced to the country that Great Britain had declared war against Germany. Two days before, Germany had invaded Poland. During his address to the nation, he said:

Up to the very last it would have been quite possible to have arranged a peaceful and honourable settlement between Germany and Poland, but Hitler would not have it. He had evidently made up his mind to attack Poland whatever happened, and although he now says he put forward reasonable proposals which were rejected by the Poles, that is not a true statement. The proposals were never shown to the Poles, nor to us, and, although they were announced in a German broadcast on Thursday night, Hitler did not wait to hear comments on them, but ordered his troops to cross the Polish frontier.

His action shows convincingly that there is no chance of expecting that this man will ever give up his practice of using force to gain his will. He can only be stopped by force.

We and France are today, in fulfilment of our obligations, going to the aid of Poland, who is so bravely resisting this wicked and unprovoked attack on her people. We have a clear conscience. We have done all that any country could do to establish peace. The situation in which no word given by Germany's ruler could be trusted and no people or country could feel themselves safe has become intolerable. And now that we have resolved to finish it, I know that you will all play your part with calmness and courage.

Douglas returned from his first voyage at the end of July 1939. He embarked on his second journey on 11 August, again heading for Australia.

He had just arrived in Colombo, Sri Lanka (then Ceylon), the day that war was announced. By this time, he was a crew member on SS *Ormonde*, which with berths for 1,560, was every bit as large as her sister ship, the *Oronsay*. He was employed again as a steward but with two jobs this time – he was a bathroom and wine steward. 'Immediately,' he recalled upon being told about the declaration of war, 'we fell under the orders of the Royal Navy, and the first thing we did was black out our portholes.'

It was fortuitous that he had requested to be allowed to change to this vessel. He had done so because three of his friends – Jimmy Lawson from Beccles, Jack Winter from Leiston and Tommy Trundle from Lowestoft – all crewed on *Ormonde* and Douglas simply felt life on board ship would be a 'whole lot better with my mates'. It was not the easiest decision, however, because the departure date of *Ormonde's* journey was over a week earlier than that of *Oronsay*, and by this time he had become engaged to Violet, a close and 'very pretty' friend of his sister, Marjorie:

> Violet was upset at my leaving so soon after coming back from my first trip. But as it turned out it was a decision that could have saved my life. On 9th October 1942 SS *Oronsay* sank after being struck by two torpedoes, whilst in the Atlantic off the west coast of Africa. Thankfully many crew were rescued, but six died. Terrible …

Douglas didn't change ship again throughout the rest of the war, serving on SS *Ormonde* as a steward until his discharge from the Merchant Navy in October 1945. His continuous Certificate of Discharge lists fifteen engagements between April 1939 and June 1945, after which he had to take sick leave. His wartime service saw him cover thousands of sea miles, sometimes to the east, to Australia twice, America, Africa and often into Europe. Being on board a troopship, he met and helped with the collection of hundreds of troops, and also hundreds of prisoners.

Some of these trips he was able to recall in far greater detail than others. Not surprisingly, the distances, places, miles and memories of his travels have become confused – they have merged into an ocean of their own. Like the sea always moves, during his years in the navy, Douglas was always on the move too, and no two days were ever the same. It was undoubtedly a very hard life indeed, but one that was as fulfilling as it was fearful, full of surprises, camaraderie – and pain, both mental and physical.

Below are some memories that are still vivid, some of which are written up in his biography, which has been lovingly put together by his niece, Pat. In sharing this part of his life with me, he is telling his story while also telling the story of his Merchant Navy comrades, friends for whom he had the deepest respect, and not a day goes by that he does not think of them.

However, Douglas's experience and recollection is not limited to those he served with on SS *Oronsay* and *Ormonde*. In finding the courage and strength to look back as he has done for this book, he has done a great service to all those who served in the Merchant Navy during the Second World War. The Merchant Navy was not a large force compared to other fighting services. It had a contingent of around 185,000 during the war years, around a quarter of whom died at sea. Douglas Huke's memory is a tribute to all of them.

★★★

'Tea! Lots of it too!' Douglas said, as he reflected on key moments of his first voyage on SS *Ormonde*. 'That's what we bought in Colombo; the day war was announced. We spent what little money we had on lovely tea, to take back home.'

By this point during her journey, SS *Ormonde* had taken her crew to Gibraltar, then into the Mediterranean past France and Italy, before sailing on to Port Said in Egypt and Oran, in Algeria, where they 'bunkered' for a while until she was refuelled with gallons more oil. Then *Ormonde* took Douglas and the crew to Suez, before their very memorable stop in Colombo.

After Sri Lanka, they continued on towards Australia and, after reaching Brisbane, Douglas remembers 'turning around and going to Sydney, heading for the naval base in Cockatoo Island', where hundreds of British and colonial convicts were held in the mid-nineteenth century. He said:

It was here that I thought I was going to lose me hearin'! We had no passengers at the time and the Captain suddenly said, 'Well, we've got a gun, so we're going to fire the gun'! And he did, and it nearly shook the poor old ship to kingdom come! She was a 1906 ship, she couldn't take it, I thought she was going to fall to pieces. But after that he threatened to shoot another one – the first one was a 6 inch gun that had been fitted to the 'aft poop deck', and the second one was going to be a 3.5 inch anti-aircraft gun, fitted to the promenade deck. It was only when one of the crew pointed out to the captain that if he did let it go again, we'd probably lose one, or even both, of our funnels; and he held back.

What a journey it was. We collected some passengers, but the only cargo we took in Australia were crates of skinned rabbits; which we put in the freezer. We offered them to everyone we met at all the ports we stopped in, including Algiers, the Philippines and Malta – but nobody wanted them! We would have given them to anyone who would take them … we only managed to get rid of the damn rabbits when we got back to Tilbury!

The next voyage Douglas recalled was not such a lengthy trip, but a very important one – and potentially very dangerous – because of the intense presence of the German High Seas Fleet, who were equipped with torpedo-bearing submarines. *Ormonde*'s charter on this occasion – despatched on 30 May 1940 – was to sail from Tilbury to Scapa Flow in Orkney, from where she was to sail to Narvik in Norway, to collect Polish soldiers.

The Poles needed rescuing after being captured by the Germans, who they had been battling in the mountains surrounding this north Norwegian city, as part of the Norwegian campaign of the Second World War. It was here, Douglas said, that he feared for his life. 'I never thought we would get through,' he said.

However, before this journey even began, Douglas recalled to me how he had learnt of the order that he was to be part of this crew:

> I'd only been on dry land for about a day. I hadn't even got home; Violet had come to meet me at the docks at Oulton Broad, and while we were on the bus heading home, I saw my sister riding past, on a bicycle, waving a telegram. So I got off the bus and found it was a message telling me to go back. So I had to return the following day.
>
> When we got to Scapa Flow, we were told we were going to go to Norway to collect as many troops and prisoners as we could. But before we left something amazing happened – the Aurora Borealis – I saw the northern lights! The midnight sun – it was really, really wonderful.

The beauty of the northern lights was a stark contrast to the horror of what Douglas was shortly to experience. SS *Ormonde* was one of a number of Royal and Merchant Navy vessels involved in the rescue and ongoing campaign where the enemy was putting up a strong defence. Douglas wrote in his memoir, 'German ships came on to us all night, even though we had the cruisers HMS *Sheffield* and *Ark Royal* as our escorts. A tanker and an armed trawler were sunk, and SS *Orama* was shot at and torpedoed.' Nineteen of *Orama*'s crew of 300 were drowned; the remainder, including the captain, were taken prisoner.

Ormonde eventually began her return with twenty-three happily rescued Polish POWs. Douglas wrote:

> At home in Lowestoft Vi thought I had been captured. She did not know I was on the *Ormonde* and was safe. We got out by zig-zagging and made our way back to Birkenhead. Moving along in a zig-zag made us safer because it was harder for us to be hit from above or below.

At Birkenhead, instead of carrying troops, *Ormonde* was loaded up with dynamite – around 20 tonnes – for the purposes of blowing up bridges in France. Over 100 engineers joined the crew, in order to carry out the explosions.

It was now the middle of June in 1940. France had not quite yet surrendered, but Belgium, the Netherlands and Luxembourg were all occupied, and France had all but fallen. The evacuation of British troops from Dunkirk had taken place a couple of weeks before; albeit a more successful evacuation than those planning and orchestrating it dared hope for, but one which also left hundreds of men still needing to be brought home.

Germany was resolute in its determination to take France as soon as possible and Churchill, who had succeeded Neville Chamberlain as prime minister on 10 May 1940, was resigned to the imminent surrender of France. He wanted British troops home – alive – to fight in the Battle of Britain. So, after delivering the explosives *Ormonde* was sent to France to assist with the evacuation of some of the remaining troops.

It was then, on 17 June 1940, that Douglas witnessed the awfulness of war in a way that he has remembered ever since. On board *Ormonde*, he sailed into the harbour of St Nazaire off the west coast of France, to where hundreds of British Expeditionary Force troops were making their way to be collected by a number of ships, including *Ormonde*.

One of the ships – possibly the largest – the *Lancastria*, was hit by three bombs as it was docked in the harbour. Precise records as to the number of those who died have never been established because there was no official record of those on board, but it has been said that there were as many as 9,000 of which fewer than 2,500 survived. Most were troops, but there were also refugees – men, women and children from France, Belgium and Holland seeking escape from the horror of German occupation.

Douglas cried as he recalled what he saw that day, after the three bombs hit *Lancastria*, one of which went straight down one of the funnels. He said:

> It was a terrible sight. All the oil tanks caught fire and the oil in the sea was set alight, and all people could do was jump into the blazing water. Another ship, the *Orford*, picked up some of the survivors – people of all ages, maimed and burnt, with arms and legs missing.

Douglas told me that the master of the *Orford* left the harbour as soon as he could – before receiving orders to do so – knowing that his passengers urgently needed the medical attention they could get in England. But Churchill ordered that the bombing of *Lancastria* was not to be made public, and the master of the *Orford* was court-martialled for disobeying Board of Trade rules; something that Douglas felt was shockingly unfair.

Winston Churchill had his reasons for ordering that the tragedy of *Lancastria* should be kept as secret as possible. Principally, almost certainly for what the knowledge could have done to the morale of those preparing for the next fight, the forthcoming Battle of Britain. However, what a legacy of sadness such secrecy leaves; hundreds (if not thousands) of families left ignorant as to the demise of their loved ones.

Even today, few people are aware of the sinking of the *Lancastria*, even though it is now acknowledged to be – in terms of the number of those who died – the worst maritime disaster in history. Douglas's memory and recall of this event, therefore, serves as a tribute to all of those who died that day. Once again, I write, as I have done so many times throughout the chapters of this precious book, that this memory is very important. Without accounts such as Douglas's, many minds would remain closed to the knowledge of such a tragedy. We need to know and care about our history. It is thanks to the courage of veterans such as Douglas that at least we have an opportunity to do that.

Douglas's, and the *Ormonde's*, next destination was Iceland. They sailed to the capital, Reykjavík, via Birkenhead, where the troops they had brought home were dropped off. He recalled spending about twelve days in Iceland, dropping off around 150 soldiers and, after coming back to England again, going on leave for four days, during which he went home to Vi and, at last, on 27 July 1940 they were able to get married.

Douglas told me how, soon after he got home, he rushed to a tailor and quickly had a suit 'knocked up' for his big day. Vi's sisters, Kathleen and Maude were bridesmaids, together with his sister, Marjorie. They snatched two nights away for their honeymoon at a boarding house in Norwich, during which time they went to a pub together – having half a pint of beer each – the first time they had been out for a drink on their own. Their marriage lasted for fifty-nine and a half years. Sadly, Vi died in January 2000.

★★★

The next couple of pages of Douglas's chapter are taken directly from his story which was given to his niece, Pat, in 2016. Then he was 99 years old, looking forward to his 100th birthday and suddenly compelled by the passing of time to write up his story. In his own words, here is what he has written about his last five years of the Second World War:

> I returned to Birkenhead on Monday 29th July 1940, and left for Freetown, Accra and Takoradi. We took troops into Cape Town, South Africa and many were sick with influenza. The sick had to be taken off and dispatched to the army hospital in Durban for two weeks. While we were in Durban waiting for troops to re-embark, my friend Winter and I went ashore for a few

drinks. We started off with Castle lager, then onto another bar and ordered brandy and ginger. A few other mates came in and plenty of rounds were consumed. Later, Winter wanted to move to another bar and ordered more beer. I felt unwell and asked him to get me a taxi back to the ship, but he got a rickshaw instead. All the bumping up and down in the rickshaw made me very ill indeed. I vowed not to do that again!

We then sailed up to Mombasa; Winter was sick and put ashore. Then we went onto Bombay to disembark troops. Afterwards, we sailed back to Mombasa to pick up Winter, and returned via Cape Town to Liverpool. A Lieutenant in the troops was the son of the landlady of the Lord Nelson public house at the top of Kimberley Road, in Lowestoft, and when I got back home, I gave her a message from her son; I was so pleased to do that. It meant she knew her son was well.

We then did an unescorted trip to Boston, Massachusetts, then on to Halifax, Nova Scotia, picking up Canadian troops to bring them back to Glasgow. I was just back from the Tropics and on the morning watch from 2 am to 4 am, with no extra winter clothing provided I nearly froze to death! We arrived back in December 1940. Glasgow customs would not let the Canadian troops disembark. They wanted a drink, so they broke into the bondage store to get it; they were all fined, about £1,000 in total. But they got their drink.

In January 1941 the *Ormonde* had a refit in Glasgow. But it didn't get much more comfy for us! We still slept about six of us to a cabin; and still only had a rough, cold old place to go to for our showers. I hated those showers! And it was bloody hard work, cleaning lots of bathrooms and also going into the saloon at lunchtime to pour wine for the captain.

Anyway, after the refit *Ormonde* was sent to Loch Fyne to be used for training commandos. But the training was cancelled, and we went to Birkenhead to have paravanes fitted. [These are torpedo-shaped devices towed from the bow of a vessel so that the cables will cut the anchors of moored mines, causing the mine to rise to the surface, so it can be destroyed or removed from the water.]

Then we went to Bombay, quite an empty ship, to pick up Australian and New Zealand troops who had been brought over on the RMS (Royal Mail Ships) *The Queen Mary* and the *Mauretania*. We picked up a lot of troops in Bombay, and also loaded up with a lot of goat's meat (it was a horrible sight). A New Zealand soldier asked me, 'What is that bloody stuff?' and when I told him exactly what it was and that it was 'lovely!', he said 'I'm not eating that!'

We anchored in the Bay of Bombay, waiting for orders to go, but the New Zealanders took control and would not let us leave, because they hated the idea of eating the goat's meat. Their language was dreadful! Eventually, negotiations began and finally it was agreed that all the meat should be dumped overboard, at night, into the sea. So into the water it all went, whilst we headed to Port Tewfik at the end of the Suez Canal. But because we had dumped the meat, we only had corned beef and potatoes. Water was scarce and limited, too, so sea water was used for showers and bathing.

But, goat's meat aside, Douglas had huge respect for the Kiwis. He said they were 'so, so brave. They had been in prisoner-of-war camps and had had horrible times.' But there was still much to be done, and those who were strong enough were taken to Egypt. This delivery of troops continued until late 1942 – by which time Field Marshal Montgomery was ready to launch the Second Battle of Al Alamein.

Finally, after many months of troop delivery, in the middle of May 1943 the Allies, led by 'Monty' Montgomery, Field Marshal Alexander and General Sir Kenneth Anderson, successfully brought about the end of the campaign in North Africa, with the (albeit painful) victory in Tunisia. After this, Douglas, still bathroom and wine steward, travelled to Sicily and Italy via Algeria. After dropping troops in Taranto (in Italy), they were ordered back to Algeria to collect German prisoners, who they then brought back to England to be held captive here.

★★★

SS *Ormonde* proved herself to be a true workhorse of the sea before, during and after the Second World War. The threat presented by Germany with their U-boats and torpedoes would have been forever in the minds of those serving in the navy throughout the war, including of course those in the British Merchant Navy Fleet. Throughout the war, with the extent of their armoury, the Germans demonstrated that they considered U-boat warfare extremely important to winning the war because of our reliance on seaborne supplies.

Douglas has not recorded the moments of true fear that could be expected for one who served for as long and with as much loyalty and dedication as he. However, there can be no doubting the courage required to simply serve for this long, in waters which were often mined and in the knowledge that a torpedo-bearing submarine might be just around the corner. 'Oh yes, we were always aware of the dangers,' he said, 'but on board the ship, well we just got on with it.'

He has, however, written about the safety drill, which all Merchant Navy seaman would have learned and which undoubtedly saved some lives. However, it was far from foolproof. It was called 'Abandon Ship Practice'. Douglas recalled one dry run, which took place at the Firth of Clyde, in Glasgow:

The lifeboats were in two tiers, layer boats and nesting boats. We dropped off the layer boats and tried to haul up the davits [small cranes used to raise and lower the lifeboats], but they twisted around and would not come up. After trying for about one and half hours, the order was abandoned. We were sent ashore to get some sandbags to weigh the davits down in case they were needed in the future. There was a life raft on skids that would accommodate a hundred of us, and the following day the order was given 'Chocks away.' But nothing happened. We should have just slid into the water. Hammers, wedges etc. were used but still nothing happened, and the order was abandoned, and we never tried again. We always had to wear life-jackets and slept with them beside our beds. We only had three minutes if we were torpedoed, and half the life-jackets were useless too.

Gratitude must always be awarded to Douglas and his comrades, thousands of whom are represented by his telling his story to me, because, in the words of the Right Honourable Alfred Barnes, Minister of War Transport during a speech in the House of Commons on 30 October 1945:

The Merchant Seaman never faltered. To him we owe our preservation and our very lives. The thanks of this House be accorded to the officers and men of the Merchant Navy for the steadfastness with which they maintained our stocks of food and materials; for their services in transporting men and munitions to all the battles over all the seas, and for the gallantry with which, though a civilian service, they met and fought the constant attacks of the enemy.

5

DRIPPING TAP
– FRED HOOKER

Fred was in Bomber Command; a rear gunner on Halifaxes. This is his memory of being shot down – capture, interrogation, prisoner-of-war days, the Long March and the return home.

Fred Hooker, taken in June 2018. He's holding the RAF baton, marking the centenary of the RAF. (Sean Strange/Daniel Shepherd)

Arriving at a wire strand fence, one of the two guards escorting me held the bottom wire down with his boot and I crawled between the wires and, like any English gentleman, waited for them to follow me. One wriggled through, as I had done, and stood intimidatingly close to me. He turned, stared, and suddenly, to my surprise, I felt a Jack-boot where it hurts. The pain of that moment has never really gone away. Every time I recall it shivers go up my spine. Needless to say, I didn't stop walking again until I had to climb on board a bus.

It was on a cold, damp autumn day in September 1944 that Fred Hooker was captured by German officers and taken away to be a POW. He was captured after bailing out of the four-engine Halifax bomber in which he was the mid-upper gunner, after it was attacked en route to marshalling yards (railway stations housing mostly carriages of freight) in Münster, in the west of Germany, where his flight had been instructed to drop their bombs:

We had had the green light from control and were soon on our way flying over the North Sea. Phil (the pilot) mentioned that he couldn't get the height we should be flying at which was 19,000 ft. He could only make 18,500 ft – after a small discussion it was decided to carry on at that height, not go lower. We encountered a small amount of flak heading towards Münster.

But alas the next thing I knew was sitting in my turret in fresh air. There was no perspex around me at all and my Browning guns were trailing over the rear turret and ammunition was being pulled from the container following the guns. I can remember disconnecting my oxygen so I could get out of the turret thinking I would go up front as I had no verbal contact with anyone and no guns! I also remember thinking it felt long since I had heard voices over the intercom. I think I had also been knocked out by an exploding shell or shells, but the air brought me round.

I stepped down into the fuselage into a mass of flames towards the rear of the aircraft, saw someone go out through the hatch, picked up my parachute that was on fire, and threw it back down again. Being without oxygen I think was beginning to affect me. I remember seeing Charlie (the flight engineer) coming towards me as I just stood there. He picked up my parachute, put his arms across the flames, clipped the chute on and pushed me out. The last person I saw before my exit was Phil, as white as a sheet, control stick hard in his stomach; then I was gone.

The next thing I remember was floating down to earth, rather too quickly, I suspect not having a complete parachute made me go quite fast. I could see another one going down and our air-craft going away in full blaze. I could see lots of people running to the field I was about to land in. While floating down, I saw a Spitfire flying very low, circling around me. The pilot flipped his wings a couple of times several hundred feet from the ground then climbed away very steeply. The Spitfire was one in a flight from Kent that had been our escort on our mission to Münster. As I neared the ground a few shots echoed in the air and I won-dered; what was going to happen?

On seeing what I thought were German troops I stood up with hands held high. It was 6.30 p.m., still daylight and no chance of escape. The soldiers did keep the civilians away other-wise I might not be here today.

The following day I was reunited with Charlie, and Taffy our bomb aimer. It was that day that our worst fears were realised. Phil and Leslie, our tail gunner, had perished in the aircraft. The guard seemed quite moved as he told us. He said we shouldn't be fighting each other but should be together against the Russians. Then he turned and left us in our cell.

Fred's recollection of this memory is important because it describes what was a frightening reality for so many and in reading his words we can begin to try and appreciate – at least a little bit – the horrifying circumstances they experienced in protection of our country. They suffered excruciating physical pain from gunshot wounds, starvation, burning, exhaustion and bruising, accompanied by the emotional pain of grief, fear, uncertainty, isolation – for many, time and time and time again. Air Force, Army, Navy – whatever their sphere of service, by being part of it, physical and emotional suffering at any moment could be just around the corner.

I always think it is strange to say, 'We must remember' because, of course, we were not there and we can't remember something we were not part of, but we must try and appreciate what men like Fred experienced on our behalf. In reading his words, we can at least try to do that. From his recollection we can take strength, courage and resilience. What Fred went through that day – and for the weeks that followed which will shortly be described – encompassed so much of what so many thousands experienced, but at least now Fred can look back with pride, and no regrets. He was part of a war that he wanted to win. We need to be thankful for what he did, as do future generations – and be grateful for Fred's willingness to share his story now, enabling our deeper understanding of this war.

As I listened to Fred tell me his story, I simply felt so deeply for him. He had been so close to dying himself. Two out of seven in his crew did perish – he witnessed their deaths as he fell to the ground. I expect 'survivor's guilt' took hold, even from that moment, deep in his subconscious. In some ways, his survival (and that of Charlie and Taffy) could be described as a miracle, however, nothing can demonstrate more clearly that the moment of our death is out of our control. We die when we die.

Back to Fred's story – the day of his capture after hastily landing in enemy territory in a field of lumpy, hard bulbs of sugar beet. After getting to his feet that evening, all he could do was keep going, compliant in the situation that had been forced upon him.

He was comforted very slightly, however, he told me, by the protection he knew should be afforded to him by the Geneva Convention, the relevant parts of which had been drilled into him during his training. This was a treaty which, in part, stipulated how POWs should be looked after upon capture and in subsequent captivity. Both Germany and Britain were signatories to this Convention, which didn't offer guarantees, of course. The theatre of war is a cruel and unpredictable place but at least this protective treaty did exist. The German officers would have known they would be at risk of harsh punishment if they acted in ways contrary to the rules of the Convention.

Therefore, at least Fred knew, while marching through the drizzle, aching furiously with every step, that the German officers were not allowed – under the rules of the Convention – to: (i) confiscate any possessions (other than weapons (which he didn't have), or a horse (which he also did not have!); (ii) deprive him of food to the point of starvation as a form of punishment; and (iii) interrogate him to the point of torture. He was only obliged to give them his date of birth, service number, rank and name.

Fred walked with the guards for a few hours, after which he was hugely relieved to be reunited with Charlie and Taffy, both of course as wretchedly confused and bruised as Fred. The three were instructed to board a small train, at which point they were banned (in no uncertain terms) from talking to each other at all. Fred learned this the hard way. He received a painful rap on his wrists after trying to shake Charlie's hand.

The train took the three of them to a large, dismal recreation hall somewhere in Münster. Nothing much happened in the hall, Fred said, but they were not allowed to communicate. Most of what Fred recalled while they were forced to stand and wait (not knowing for what) in that hall was the physical weakness of Taffy who, out of the three of them, was in the most pain. Fred just wanted to give him an arm, but he was not allowed to. Fred clearly loathed being unable to support his friend.

After a short while in the hall, together with the guards, Fred told me how he, Charlie and Taffy were then ordered to:

> … half-march, half-walk along a canal bank where people were getting furniture out of burning houses. The houses were burning furiously, and we were told (by the guards) that it was 'our bombs' that had done the damage. We were attacked a number of times by civilians with broom handles and sticks hitting us across our backs, not a pleasant experience by any means.

Eventually the march concluded at some army barracks and together they were put into a cell where they spent the next couple of days. It was a room with only a bench, but at least they could rest. A slice of black bread was all they received to eat. It was 'revolting' at first, Fred said, but as it partially staved off their hunger, they started to quite enjoy it.

The next stage of their captive journey was a twenty-eight-hour train journey to an interrogation centre in a place called Frankfurt-on-Main. Fred had been told about such centres back in England, during his training. They were nicknamed 'rooms without a bath', and he recalled the instruction that if they were to end up at such a place to be on guard as much as possible and mention only rank, name and number.

After being put into a cell on his own, it was here that Fred first felt very alone and 'cut off from the rest of the world', fearing he might never see the people he knew and loved ever again. For days he didn't even know if Taffy and Charlie were in the same building.

Fred was stuck in this cell for over two weeks, the only conversation being the interrogation he was periodically subjected to. The questioning was bad enough, said Fred – questions were fired at him by one guard, while another pointed a pistol at his head – but it was the 'dripping tap torture' that Fred really hated. For two weeks he craved a drink of water but the only liquid he received was contained in the meagre rations of bread and a grassy 'soup' that they were periodically given. There was a lever-style contraption in his room that he could lower to call a guard when he needed to relieve himself. He told me:

> When I used to drop the arm for attention for the toilet, on being ushered next door, I would always try and get a drink of water, but I was always stopped, although a tap was dripping night and day. What torture that was.

To this day, seventy-four years later, he still hates the noise of water dripping from a tap.

It was a relief to Fred when the hell of the interrogation centre finally ended. Although he was moving to a POW camp, at least he would be released from his isolation. On the day of departure from the interrogation centre, he was reunited with Taffy and Charlie and joined by other British servicemen on the same journey.

A train was to take them to the camp, and on the way they stopped at a transit station called Wetzlar, where their spirits were considerably lifted. He said, 'In today's terms, it would be like going from our bungalow to the Ritz Hotel!' They were reminded of genuine human kindness in the form of Red Cross parcels containing clean clothes and toiletries, and for the first time in days they were given meals that reminded them that food could still be worth tasting. He said:

> We were given a small case with new clothing and towels inside; three pairs of underpants, three singlets, shirts, socks, towels, soap and shaving equipment, and taken to the shower room. This was the first time since leaving England that I had water on my body

and how I enjoyed that shower. I can still remember the feeling also of having new clean clothing on and a nice thick blue pullover on top and to be able to comb my hair and shave. After all of this, we sat down for a meal and the thing I remember most was a big plateful of corned beef and mashed potatoes, all mixed together. I remotely remember tinned fruit for pudding and a good mug of tea.

It was from Wetzlar that Fred was first able to make contact with his family, through completing a Red Cross letter form. He wasn't able to write very much, because of the threat of scrutiny by the Germans, but his own script declaring that he was alive would have been all that mattered. Up until then he had been posted as 'missing' and that is what his parents had been told.

After a few days at Wetzlar, Fred began the next stage of his POW journey; a fairly non-eventful but tedious bus ride to Stalag Luft VII, their destination camp in the south-western (now Polish) town of Bankau. Prior to the journey, he was grateful to receive an American Red Cross parcel containing tinned meat, powdered milk, prunes, emergency ration chocolate, sugar, coffee and dried egg. On arrival at Stalag VII, he was forced to march for a while before his photograph and fingerprints were taken.

Fred continued to be grateful to Charlie; they had managed to stick together throughout and this continued for the duration of their captivity in Bankau. There was very little accommodation to speak of. Established to house RAF non-commissioned officers, within a month of opening in June 1944 it held 230 prisoners and by January 1945 it held nearly 1,600. These were captives of many nationalities – predominantly British, but also Australians, Canadians, South Africans, Dutch and French. When they arrived in September 1944, it was already becoming fearfully overcrowded, prisoner numbers having swelled considerably after the Battle of Arnhem, which presented Germany with a much-needed victory, due in part to the strength of their powerful Panzer tanks, which successfully blocked off the Arnhem Road Bridge in the Netherlands.

Charlie and Fred's 'bedroom', initially, was a nothing more than draughty garden shed which they shared with five others. They slept on thin layers of brown paper, in between which they laid wood shavings. They were locked in throughout the night and were only allowed to leave one at a time to use the 'bathroom'. When nature called, they indicated their need to a guard with a lever system similar to that at the interrogation centre. The lavatory, Fred said, was 'out of this world'; a huge trench dug out, on which the user had to balance oneself above on a large pole, with holes drilled into it. It was quite a sight, he said – especially when there was a 'full house'. It doesn't bear to think of the consequences of toppling off the pole.

Slowly, Fred settled into life as a POW. Each day was long, uncomfortable and cold, but not once did he indicate bitterness about the time he spent there, instead generously describing his time in the camp as 'reasonable'. He spoke a lot of his developing friendship with Charlie, and of others with whom he formed a close bond. He mentioned especially two sergeants, Tommy Veitch and Frank Veid – a gunner and an engineer, respectively. He also spoke kindly of a couple of Canadians, a 'wee Scots lad' and a Kiwi, who eventually married Charlie's younger sister.

There was little to break the tedium of their daily routine except a nervous apprehension always that something far worse could be just around the corner that kept them on their toes. He said:

We learnt to pass some time away during the day by walking around the perimeter of the compound being sure not to go over the trip wire, which, if I remember correctly was about six feet away from the main fence. The fence was mainly horrible barbed wire coils in between two main fences and about

14 feet high. The top was inward sloping, to make it extremely difficult to get over. Every so many yards, I'm not sure of the exact distance, a sentry lookout post was positioned on high posts with a large searchlight which was used to sweep all over the camp in case of an attempted escape.

Fred told me of something that happened that was quite extraordinary. It was not what we would expect at all for POWs, but very special and, for want of a better word, quite amazing. It involved his teeth. Within about three weeks of his stay at Stalag VII he was invited, together with other prisoners, to notify the medical officer if they needed dental treatment (I can only imagine most of them did!). Fred thought he might as well ask for as much as possible and requested an almost completely new set of teeth. He received his new 'teeth' in exchange for a bar of soap, which he was glad to relinquish.

Christmas at Stalag VII is one that has long been imprinted on his memory. By this time, he and his comrades had discovered the merits of pooling their food rations. For example, instead of devouring the moderate but welcome edible items of their Red Cross parcels individually, they shared them out together, which gave more variety – and exercised their imaginations too, as they created different 'recipes'. There was more than one way of mixing tinned meat with potato skins, for example:

> Christmas lunch between us was a pudding consisting of crusts of bread we had saved for a few days and crumbled, dry biscuits also crumbled, prunes and sultanas cut up very finely, dried egg and dried milk powder, all mixed with water.

He said he could remember the mixture his mother used to make, and they end up with a little pudding which was quite solid, 'nice and firm'. Cooked ingeniously on a stove fuelled by wood shavings, over which they laid scraps of wood, they placed the pudding in an old empty powdered milk tin, which they suspended over their small fire. The pudding was served with cream they made from powdered milk and it was simply 'terrific', Fred declared. He called the stove the 'blower', and with it, they could also make tea, coffee and 'light the occasional cigarette'.

By Christmas, the prisoners had worked out a number of ways of passing the time. He said that sometimes he would 'listen to different chaps giving talks on a variety of subjects, such as Peter, an Australian who loved to talk about the sheep he farmed before he left them behind, and another who educated me about Suffolk punches'. He said that at Christmas:

> A group of chaps put on a stage show and had dresses, etc. Nothing of this went on without the Germans being present and some of the guards had a good laugh, too. One thing that kept the spirits of us chaps up was regular news of how the war was going and this was obtained by a secret crystal radio which one of the longer serving POWs had. While the news was being broadcast by the BBC, notes were made and the message read out in different huts, very secretively, and sharp lookout kept for approaching 'ferrets' (German guards) who were walking around the camp all the time.

It wasn't long after Christmas that rumours began to abound that Russian forces had begun their westward advance, which the POWs knew would almost certainly result in their departure from the camp. The rumours were not groundless; after a false alarm on 17 January during which they were ordered to gather in the parade ground with their few personal belongings, they were ordered back to barracks, and simply had to wait for further instructions. Finally, suddenly, in the freezing cold of the night on 19 January 1945, at 3.30 a.m. genuine marching orders were given.

Together with around 1,600 other captive comrades, Fred was instructed to leave the camp. He did – and there began their 'Long March' home. The harsh conditions of Stalag Luft VII were nothing compared to what they faced during this part of his war. Each and every one of them – those who were able to keep going, many did not – endured hunger and exhaustion, while having to cope with the very bitter, challenging weather, which resulted in many cases of hypothermia and frostbite. Survival was the name of the game. Some of those who struggled and held the troops back were shot in the back of the head. The German officers were present and very much in charge. Determined to keep ahead of the Russians, no one was allowed to slow them down.

Accompanied by Charlie and other close friends, including Tommy and Frank, Fred's march continued much as it had begun. Fred said:

> Before leaving, we were issued with rations for two and [a] half days. The weather was terrible and very, very cold. We arrived at a place called Winterveldt. We had covered a distance of 28 kilometres and our resting place was a barn on a farm with cold floors, with just a bit of hay.
>
> On 20th January, we were on the road again at 5 a.m. It was snowing … eventually we were allowed to rest again at about 10 a.m., this time at an old disused brickworks. Just imagine hundreds of us, jostling for a place out of the wind to rest (and find a place for nature comforts.) When it got dark, we were ordered to move on.

Then came Fred's coldest, most fearful night of all. Still with Charlie, Tommy and Frank, they trudged through snow almost waist high, during the night, in temperatures of -20 degrees. With two pairs of socks on his hands instead of gloves and thin blankets instead of a proper coat, the cold almost defeated them, Fred included. Someone had found some wood at the brickworks and had the ingenuity to take it for use as a sledge. It was only big enough for their belongings but was still a small help.

However, then Fred recalled a moment of complete immobility. He said:

> All four of us were sitting on our sledge with not another person in sight. The road ahead was smooth, the wind blowing, the snow flattened by 1,500 other men, I can't recall any conversation between us, until then we had been moving very slowly, helping each other along, but suddenly we just reached a standstill. How long we sat I have no idea. We couldn't, and didn't move, but then we did. I do believe that, to this day, 'Somebody' gave us the strength and will power to move on.

There followed something of a rush to reach the next stage of their journey – a bridge that crossed the River Oder, a wide and fast-running river that traversed Germany's border with Poland. Rumours were rife among the column of miserably cold marching prisoners that those who did not reach this bridge by a certain time would be left to the mercy of the advancing Russians.

Struggling through the snow, slipping on ice and closing their eyes to blizzards, somehow most – but not all – reached the bridge. After walking for less than a mile after reaching the other side, the Germans, as good as their word, blew up the bridge.

Then, at last some rest. For two days they were afforded respite – although peace of mind in the conditions they were being forced to endure was very far away. Their 'resting place' was a cow barn and, while the hay was plentiful, so too was cattle excrement. It was a huge relief, said Fred, to at least be able to take off their boots which were frozen solid. Before trying to sleep there was much rubbing of feet to try and get the blood circulating.

This rest, of sorts, was rudely ended at 3 a.m. on 22 January. There was panic among the German guards that the Russians had sped up their advance and they were forced to begin the next stage of the march – and begin it very quickly. Again, survival was the name of the day. Those who wanted to survive had to do as they were told.

Conditions continued to be absolutely horrendous and because they had nothing – at all – to eat they had started to forage for whatever they could, some of them managing to take in mouthfuls of raw sugar beet and rhubarb. This led to horrendous stomach pain and stomach upsets. Others ate rats, even cats and dogs, if they could catch them and had the energy to kill them. It wasn't very long before many were suffering as much with dysentery and diarrhoea as starvation, and the biting cold – temperatures well below freezing with a wind-chill factor making it feel even colder – threatened hypothermia, exacerbating all their struggles.

By this time, the march had already proven to be too much for some. Those who had succumbed to the cold and were left, lifeless, in snowdrifts. Others were struggling so much that they threatened to slow down the pace of the march and were 'dealt with' by the Germans. The prisoners had to walk, and they had to walk as quickly as possible.

It wasn't until 5 February that the march ended; although it was replaced by equally torturous conditions of a different kind because the men were loaded onto cattle trucks, squashed like sardines in filthy carriages probably not fit for animals, let alone emaciated, exhausted and sick human beings. This part of their journey began in Goldberg – still quite far east, but about 100 miles from their starting point in Silesia.

Fred's main comfort was the fact that throughout all of this he, Charlie, Tommy and Frank remained together – what a much-needed boost that must have been for him. Together with around fifty other prisoners, they jostled along in these foul conditions for around three days. As they went, the stench increased because 'toilet requirements were not catered for and the small cracks by the door were soon in full use but not adequate for the number of men on board'.

However, what made the appalling state even worse was the dysentery that many of the men were suffering. Before getting into the truck someone had found a drum of what they thought was molasses, at one of the barns they had attempted to sleep in. This liquid was rapidly devoured by those who managed to put themselves at the front of the queue for it, but they were very much mistaken – it was not molasses, it was animal feed for use in silage making, and it had a very bad effect indeed on those who had consumed it.

At last, the truck reached its destination – Luckenwalde in eastern Germany, and the site of their second prisoner-of-war camp, Stalag 3A. By this time, they had been on the move for around six weeks and had covered over 140 miles. On arrival at the camp Fred said he was relieved to see huts in which he assumed they were to be accommodated, but their discomfort was set to continue. There were no beds, just lines for the men to squash up together, to attempt to sleep on paper bags which, if they were fortunate enough, were softened slightly with wood shavings. The height of luxury for them was being able to wash and shave.

At night, before a fitful sleep, delousing would take place; for most about an hour each evening would be spent looking through their underclothes catching and squeezing the unwanted, tiresome, grubby little residents. By day, they exercised – as well as marching, Fred recalled playing volleyball while others played football. They were sustained only by meagre rations of 'soup' and the occasional handful of potatoes.

As with his whole period of captivity, Stalag 3A proved to be an extremely challenging regime and many fell at this hurdle. It has since been written about as one of the toughest of all German camps. One Italian prisoner wrote afterwards that the daily food routine was for the Germans to put out a 'bucket of potatoes to be shared between twenty-five prisoners'. Many of those who collapsed through hunger were beaten for doing so.

Fred told me that those who did perish there were at least given a proper burial outside of the camp. Fred attended one of these ceremonies. He was glad to do so, but before going had to promise he would not try to escape while being outside of the wire.

It wasn't until 5 May 1945 that Fred's dark tunnel finally began to light up. American troops arrived at the camp, with vehicles to facilitate the evacuation of the prisoners and take them home. Initially, Fred had to suffer the frustration of a false alarm – the Russians would not allow the convoy to depart. However, word 'went around' that the Americans had relocated around 18km away from the camp and Fred was one of many who made an easy escape to track them down.

It was soon after this departure that Fred was treated to one of the most delicious and welcome meals that he had ever had. Just before finding the Americans, Fred was assisted by some Russian troops who guided him to a house where he was able to rest and eat. He was given bread, tinned meat and milk and a bed with cotton sheets in which to sleep.

Fred wasn't quite home, but the agonies of his long journey in captivity were over. The meal he received from a German lady, courtesy of the Russians – who ordered her to do so – was followed by the gift of a bicycle, so he could progress westwards as quickly as possible. He still had a long way to go, but he took the bike and made it to the River Elbe and crossed the bridge. There, he managed to hitch a lift with more American troops, who contacted some British servicemen who drove him to Brussels.

He was in Brussels for a couple of nights before being put on an aeroplane home. While he was there, he had plenty of food, cigarettes, drink and – most of all – company. He was one of over

15,000 troops gathered in Brussels for transport home. He was part of what became known as Operation Exodus – a Bomber Command initiative to bring the men home. At last the war, at least in this part of Europe, was over.

Fred was flown back in a Dakota – a treat for him because he had never been in one before and, as the only RAF member on board, he was delighted to be invited into the cockpit. On departure from the plane, he was equally delighted and surprised to be received by a high-ranking military officer, who gave him a really 'hearty handshake'. Even after everything he had been through, Fred modestly said he didn't quite understand why he deserved this.

Fred's next stop was RAF Cosford in Shropshire, which was one of the receiving stations set up to repatriate the prisoners. There, he recalled again good company and food, in addition to sleeping soundly in a comfortable bed. All the prisoners were given thorough medicals and lots of advice, and then it was home for indefinite leave. Fred took the train to Reading, almost the final leg of his long, long journey. However, much to his frustration he missed the final bus. Eventually providence prevailed for Fred, and that evening he saw a farmer friend of his who couldn't be more pleased to have the opportunity to drive their local hero home to his parents.

★★★

In learning about what it was that got the veterans who I have been privileged to talk to for the purposes of this book through the war, that friendship, trust and respect for comrades was a common theme. As Fred spoke, it was clear that his respect for those he flew with, and was subsequently imprisoned with, hasn't waned, even though the war is long since over.

While in the sky, whichever aeroplane the servicemen were in, each member of each crew had a vital role to play. For the larger aeroplanes such as the Halifax in which Fred flew, with crews of six or seven, all were dependent upon each other; the pilot was in overall control, but he was reliant upon the skill of the navigator to instruct him on the route they should take. They, in turn, had to trust their bomb aimer(s) and gunners to protect them in the event of attack, and all of them had to put their trust in the engineer whose responsibility it was to ensure their plane was flight fit and up to the job. There was no margin for error; they had to work as a team, and respect was vital.

Therefore, when Fred was reunited with Colin and Taffy on the rickety bus shortly after their captivity began, he was hugely comforted. The day their Halifax had been overcome by enemy fire was only their third bombing mission as a crew, but they had known each other for over three months, having trained together on Halifaxes, as members of 102 Squadron, based in Pocklington in Yorkshire. Fred recalled a sobering moment on his arrival in June 1944 at this rather desolate base not far from the Yorkshire dales. The remnants of a Halifax that had failed to take off properly were still scattered on the runway, and when they were shown to their billets the personal possessions of the dead crew members were still being cleared away.

However, Fred and his colleagues had to put these images to the back of their minds and get on with the tasks at hand. They had to encourage each other, pat each other on the back when things went well, commiserate and laugh when things were tough.

Fred recalled some excitement too, knowing they were in a Halifax squadron – in spite of what they had witnessed on arrival at Pocklington, the Halifax had a relatively good reputation for safety. It was a heavy bomber, featuring a large internal bomb bay, in addition to extra bombs that could be transported in the wings. It was also capable of flying much higher than most planes, giving it the reassuring capability of escaping from flak when necessary. In service with Bomber Command throughout the war, Halifax bombers flew on over 82,000 operations, during which 1,833 aircraft were lost.

By the time Fred's training was complete and his wartime combat began, it was September 1944 and 102 Squadron's principal role was to assist with the transportation of petrol to Belgium for the Second Army, who were leading the way in the liberation of occupied Belgium, determined in their capability to do so and strengthened by the recent success of the liberation, weeks earlier, of much of France.

Fred was captured after only three bombing raids – but nonetheless, he can be very proud of what he and his crew achieved in helping to liberate Belgium after the horror of its almost five-year occupation. Hopefully he is proud, too, for telling his story and enabling our understanding. Through this, so many who suffered even more than he did will be remembered, and will touch our hearts for even longer.

6

THE WEIGHING OF THE DICE
– PIERS DE BERNIÈRE-SMART

Piers was in the Queen's Bays, a cavalry regiment in the army. His chapter tells of his inspiration to be part of the war and of going into battle in Italy, after reconnaissance had been done precipitating the incursion that followed.

Piers de Bernière-Smart.
(Photo kindly given by Louis de Bernières)

By San Martino on the hill
The sickly stench of battle lingered still:
Although the crushing din had rolled away
From the grim scene of yesterday,
Its gruesome carnage lay below
The ridge from which we'd seen them bravely go
Into the flames of an explosive shell, Of armour-piercing shot
and shell.

Taken from Piers' poem 'San Martino (Montecieco) 1944', the words above tell the true story of an incompetent act that resulted in hideous emotional and physical suffering, and catastrophic loss of life. Bloody, wretched, chaotic scenes of destruction are all too commonplace in the theatre of war, but perhaps the awfulness about which Piers has written is made even worse by the fact that this poem is about 'gruesome carnage' that was avoidable.

Reconnaissance had been done and knowledge had been gathered that stated without doubt that this planned route of attack would lead to lives being lost. The innocent young men who perished that day would, I suspect, have been all too aware of that reconnaissance. These soldiers, many barely beyond late teenage years, who were loyal and dedicated to the cause, were forced to advance – as Piers has written about in another poem 'Into the Outstretched Arms of Death' – in the full knowledge of the commanders who instructed them to do so.

The event that inspired both of these poems took place on 20 September 1944, during the Battle of Coriano, in the north-east of Italy, not far from Rimini. The battle was part of the campaign to seize the Gothic Line, which stretched from La Spezia in the west of the country, through the Apennine Mountains to Ravenna in the east and was – at that stage of the war – the final main German defence of northern Italy. Rimini was critical to the German existence on that line, which featured some 2,300 machine-gun nests,

480 gun positions, concrete bunkers, barbed wire and anti-tank ditches. It was a challenging fight for both sides from its beginning in August 1944 to its completion four months later. The result was inconclusive, but even so, the Allies saw losses of some 40,000. The Gothic Line was breached throughout this time, but it wasn't until April the following year that it was finally broken.

The campaign to take this strategic line was part of the Battle of Rimini, codenamed Operation Olive. Olive was led by the British Eighth Army and the US Fifth Army. Over 1.2 million men participated and, according to Lieutenant General Oliver Leese, Commander of the Eighth Army, it was one of the toughest battles in its history. He compared the fighting to the Second Battle of El Alamein in 1942, during which some 16,000 Allies were killed, although they were nonetheless victorious and the Axis threat to Egypt was eventually brought to a halt.

Piers served at this time as a lieutenant observer in the reconnaissance troop of the Queen's Bays (the 2nd Queens Dragoon Guards), a cavalry regiment in the British Army under the 2nd Armoured Brigade. In the early hours of the morning on 20 September, the Bays positioned themselves to attack, beginning their advance to Coriano Ridge. Their orders were to capture Point 153, a defined position on the ridge. The only way to do this was to advance up a forward slope and, after reaching the ridge, proceed over it and continue to the valley opposite.

However, during the previous night, patrols of the 1st King's Royal Rifle Corps had determined the presence of the enemy all around, particularly in the valley. Aerial reconnaissance had also been undertaken, supporting their findings. The futility of the attack was obvious, even as it began, but the instructions were not withdrawn.

Initially, the Bays put up a determined and partially successful fight, demolishing some buildings on the forward slopes. But as soon as they drove over the top of the hill, they were met with devastation. They came under a storm of anti-tank fire from a series of different enemy positions. Many of the tanks were immediately shot at and officers pleaded for permission to withdraw, but they were told to continue in spite of it being abundantly clear that not only would they fail to take Point 153 but many men were doomed to be lost in the process.

As tanks were hit, crew members bailed out to avoid being burned alive inside, only to then be sniped at and machine-gunned by the enemy, many of whom were simply able to fire at them through windows from their houses. Only the few young men who managed to lie low had a chance of survival.

Piers had been seconded from C Squadron into a reconnaissance troop and had to watch the slaughter, including that of his closest friend, from an observation post where he was reporting events on a radio set.

The 9th Queens Royal Lancers, also involved in Operation Olive, were called upon to support the Bays and renew the attack, but it was too late. By the time the Lancers arrived, casualties already numbered sixty-four. The carnage took less than half an hour. A small consolation for the 'miserable day' was that the Bays attack did, at least, result in Rimini being taken by the Allies the following night.

In Piers' words:

We knew in First Armoured Division that our job was to try to penetrate the heavily fortified German Gothic Line, which terminated on the eastern side of Italy, at the city of Rimini. We had spent much of our time in southern Italy, awaiting the opportunity to make a breakthrough, getting used to armoured operations in this close country of hills and woodland, which of course had been lacking during our desert experience.

In early September 1944 we moved north to positions near the German defences of the Gothic Line and on 3rd September the initial stages of the assault on Rimini began. Progress was disheart-eningly slow, because of the appalling state of the roads and tracks we had to use, due to intense overcrowding of our military vehi-cles being on them. The countryside features made it especially difficult going for tanks. On that appalling day, 20th September 1944, the critical stage of the Battle of Coriano was reached, when First Armoured Division – of which we were a unit – were given what turned out in effect to be a suicide mission, which we had foreseen, and upon which our divisional commander had made strong representations to the commander of Five Corps.

We had to advance up our slope, where we were out of sight, over the hilltop in full view, down into the valley where we were strictly confined and where we were within a 100 yard range of the most powerful German anti-tank guns in the enemy's armoury. Our commander's (the divisional commander) objec-tions to the operation as planned were rejected and the order came from Five Corps that the advance as planned would take place immediately 'at all costs'. It was all over within 20 minutes.

If ever there was a sheer waste of life, it was that, a typical case of ambitious high command ignoring the more junior levels. We paid the costs in full, in circumstances that I attempted shortly after the event to express in poetry. I found it hard to express my feelings about in any other way.

This is the picture of the scene he painted in his poem, 'Map References':

Just a few houses on a ridge-top road:
The Ordnance map accorded it no name. Steeply below the ridge, the valley fell, A shoulder of high ground on either flank. Around the right hand shoulder, out of sight, Another fea-ture with commanding views; Another reference, Point One Five Three.

Upon the left hand shoulder, out of sight
But never out of mind in our suspense, Crouched silent anti-
tank guns on alert; Beside them, vigilant machine gun nests.
Alarmed by sounds of tanks below the ridge,
Of our assembling squadrons waiting there, Our foes were spec-
ulating how and where We would develop an assault and when.
We too were wondering what lay in store –
The critical decision 'Up at corps'

The Colonel knew.
The Brigadier knew.
The General of Division knew.
They understood the weighing of the dice:
A suicidal venture without hope
Of tactical advantage, of any kind of gain; The General made the
situation plain
But Higher Wisdom, Wedded to the Plan

Was adamant and ordered the Advance
Immediate – at all costs. The die was cast.
Over the ridge and down the forward slope
Into the outstretched Arms of Death
The Squadrons drove. All costs were paid.

Thus we were destined not to be
Possessors of Point One Five Three,
But on the ridge we crossed there stands
Our war Memorial where sands
Of time ran out. Beneath it lie
The brave who crossed the ridge to die.

Our maps were mute, we did not know
That Montecieco is the place

Where we committed to God's Grace Our fallen comrades
long ago;
And by God's Grace the people here Remember ours and
honour them Each year.

A stone's throw from our hedged, secluded place Of memory,
now spanning six decades There is a school.
Wide windows in a modern clean façade
Look down upon the peaceful countryside,
Where farms in tranquil woodland seem asleep
And hillside vineyards slumber in the sun
Of Autumn days.

Immortalised in poetry by Alfred, Lord Tennyson, the 'Charge of
the Light Brigade' (1854) is another account that tells of men carrying out orders – on this occasion on horseback – regardless of
the obvious outcome:

"Forward, the Light Brigade!"
Was there a man dismayed?
Not though the soldier knew
    Someone had blundered.
    Theirs not to make reply,
    Theirs not to reason why,
    Theirs but to do and die.
    Into the valley of Death
    Rode the six hundred.

This event refers to the charge of British light cavalry at the Battle
of Balaclava in October 1854, during the Crimean War. The intention then was to prevent the Russians from removing captured
guns from already overrun Turkish positions, but the mission failed
because of a miscommunication in the chain of command that

resulted in the Light Brigade trying to take the wrong guns. When the cavalrymen reached the artillery battery that was the target of their attack they were met by such fierce bombardment they had to retreat immediately. It was too late for many. The assault – as with Coriano Ridge – ended with high British casualties and no decisive gains. Lord Tennyson wrote his poem within six weeks of reading about it in *The Times*; possibly driven to do so by sheer dismay that young men could be so let down, possibly also at least hoping that if the disaster was recorded in this way their deaths would be remembered.

It was Piers who drew the comparison to my attention. 'Into the valley of Death,' wrote Tennyson; 'Into the outstretched Arms of Death,' wrote Piers. We – generations present and future – have a duty, I think, to take heed of these words and know that valour almost beyond our imagination scatters our history, allowing us to be where we are today. Poems such as these shouldn't just be read for their creative genius, they are critical for our knowledge and understanding.

Of the futile order to take Point 153, Piers told me too of a German general who was quoted later as saying, 'We couldn't believe our luck, when we saw you coming over the top of the hill. The tanks were prime targets. We just couldn't possibly miss.' He said it was not surprising that a German had said this because when the tanks appeared over the ridge, as they did, they were completely exposed. He compared the vulnerability of a tank in the line of fire to the vulnerability of an aircraft in the sky, exposed to anti-aircraft fire. Tanks were possibly even more vulnerable – an aeroplane at least has the advantage of speed, if it is not too damaged it can usually fly to a place of safety. The top speed of a tank counts for nothing. On this occasion, Sherman tanks were deployed, one of the mostly widely used of all Allied tanks in the war. The Germans referred to them as 'Tommy Cookers'. Generally accommodating a crew of five, they were so called because they were easily set on fire and, once alight, there was little chance of escape for those trapped inside. They were heavily armoured on the front, but on the backs and sides the armour was thin.

All of the Second World War veterans' accounts in this book feature dying and grief – some, such as Piers, saw their comrades fall with their own eyes. Others were exposed to the wider picture of death, like Flight Lieutenant Colin Bell (Chapter 7), who flew many times over the besieged city of Berlin, and thus over hundreds of buildings reduced to rubble, which he knew would have contained the bodies of those unwittingly trapped inside. Another was Fred Hooker (Chapter 5), who saw comrades succumb to freezing conditions and starvation during their 'long march' home, through northern Germany after their liberation from prisoner-of-war camps in January 1945. Finally, another poignant moment of carnage was witnessed by John Ottewell (Chapter 1), who, while in training on a beach in Devon was suddenly deafened by the noise of a German fighter flying over him, which dropped its bombs on a church hall behind him on the top of a cliff that he knew was full of schoolchildren.

With death there is grief and, perhaps out of all the accounts I have written up, it is Piers' story that has made me think most about grief and the heartfelt, bitter pain of the loved ones left behind. Countless Second World War books deal with individual battles, commanders, strategy and materiel – those who died are remembered, but the sadness of those left behind is little spoken of.

All who enter the field of war are, of course, aware of their vulnerability, the very real possibility that they might never come home. However, I don't think we think enough about those who are left behind. The fathers, mothers, sisters, brothers, cousins, wives and lovers – all whose hearts are pierced by the shocking agony of the loss of a loved one have to learn to live with the pain. The pain might waiver in its acuteness, but for most it never goes, there is no reprieve. However, if there is any comfort in the grief of those who have lost loved ones in war it can be pride. A small comfort perhaps, but at least those deeply grieving would know that their sons, lovers and brothers died in the path of the enemy, for their country and they could always be proud.

In drawing what happened at Coriano Ridge to my attention, Piers made me think of the grieving of those left behind, because these were avoidable deaths. Theirs were lives cut short in a manner in which they should not have been. In this case, yes, the Germans pulled the triggers, but how easy it was made for them to slay their vulnerable targets.

In many cases during the war, facts were not presented that could weaken the resolve of the troops and often there were cover-ups because if the information had been revealed, it might have crushed the morale of men needed for battle. So often, the truth was not revealed for many years. I don't know, but I hope and expect it was the case that the loved ones who were left behind after the tragedy at Point 153 did not know the truth about what happened that day. I hope their understanding was that their boys were overcome by a stronger enemy, on at least something of an equal battlefield.

It makes me very sad to think of those bereaved. If they had known their loved ones were so completely let down by those to whom they were entrusted, their grief would probably have been the bitterest, deepest, most painful grief of all. I asked Piers how, in the aftermath of the horror of which he had been part, he managed to go on, to continue. How do you respect your seniors after something like this? 'The deaths had to count for something,' he said. It actually presented him with a stronger, not lesser, determination to defeat the enemy. 'You just had to get on with it – there was still a war to be won.'

However, it was indelibly printed in his memory. One particular image that has stayed with him was that of his closest friend whose head he found so damaged it was barely recognisable.

Every single one of the thousands of men and women who lost their lives during the Second World War were a part of the collective courage that ultimately took us to victory. All the bones that were splintered and broken, the blood that was shed, the skin that was burnt, the torsos that were shattered, the heads that were decapitated – whatever the circumstances of death, once the hearts of those brave men and women stopped beating they, at least, were peaceful. Medal or no medal, even grave or no grave, they were heroes, and our debt of gratitude to them must endure.

Piers' poetry gives full force to the pain and carnage of that horrific day. These words are taken from another of his poems, 'Fallen Enemy 1944':

When, yesterday, I saw your swelling corpse
And bloated face
Stiff in the ditch where, in retreat, they left you
With the flies
And stinking heat, I only thought the ditch
A fitting place
For such as you. And yesterday there stung
My grieving eyes
The ghastly image of my
Mutilated friend,
Fighting to defend.
You and your kind in Field green, I loathed With all my hate
Of heart and mind. My loathing then was Hard and passionate.
Today, I hope they'll bury you; I know
You better now;
Your regiment, your name: I think
I even know the girl
You loved. Your fingers now in death's convulsions Tightly curl
Around your gun: mine found her picture.

Did she ever vow
To pray for you, to wait for you, to love you Until death?

Death, here is your sting: Life, here the vapour Of your
shallow breath.

Finally, to end this part of Piers' story, is one more verse, taken from
'Map References'. It tells of how every year, in September, school
children from the village of Montecieco, near Coriano Ridge, visit
a memorial that was erected in 1946 to remember those who died
on 20 September 1944. It is a white stone plaque, engraved with
the names of those who gave their lives will not be forgotten. The
verse is as follows:

Today, young eyes and ears would seek in vain
For sight and sound of mortal conflict here
And yet –
'Venti Settembre'
As Montecieco people say,
Is a school remembrance day,
When children and their teachers pay
Their annual tribute to a band Of soldiers from a distant land.
The children may not understand
Complexities of that past war
Which racked their village long before, But what they do here
matters more. Here, where the map accords no name,
There burns a faithful hilltop flame.

★★★

It was when he was 16, during the summer of 1940 while living
in London, that Piers first started to feel keenly the impact of
the Second World War. He was impatient to be involved, largely

inspired by the 'swarms of German bombers' he described flying overhead, heading for central London during the Battle of Britain, and later during the Blitz. He remembered seeing Luftwaffe aircraft being met by the RAF in the sky, and he thought often of the fear they must all have felt during their dogfights; crediting them for their courage, and agonising over their terror during their last moments when he saw planes falling, twisting, turning and burning, en route to their end.

Piers' determination to play his part was driven by Winston Churchill, whose speeches he particularly admired. He respected the honesty of Churchill during his first speech as prime minister (three days after succeeding Neville Chamberlain on 10 May 1940), during which he made clear the enormity of the challenges that lay ahead for the country. Churchill uttered the now famous phrase, 'I have nothing to offer but blood, toil, tears and sweat,' before going on to say, 'We have many many long months of struggling and of suffering.' He spoke, too, of his absolute resolution that we would win the war, trying to offer reassurance with the words, 'You ask, "What is our aim?" I can answer in one word. Victory, victory at all costs, victory in spite of all terror, victory however long and hard the road may be, for without victory there is no survival.' Pleading for support from the country, he said, 'Come then, let us go forward together with our united strength.'

Many people, including members of his own Cabinet, were troubled by this speech because it offered little in the way of a plan for victory, but Piers was reassured and strengthened by it. However, it wasn't until after Churchill's next speech, on 18 June 1940, during which he said, 'Let us therefore brace ourselves to our duties, and so bear ourselves that, if the British Empire and its Commonwealth last for a thousand years, men will still say, "This was their finest hour,"' that Piers' impatience ran out and – against his mother's wishes – he joined the local Air Raid Precaution (ARP) unit.

He worked as a volunteer with the ARP closest to his home, in Eltham in Kent, supporting other voluntary civilian ARP officers with the valuable work they were doing, mostly looking after members of the public during air raids. However, ARP staff also involved themselves in many other duties, and he told me about two particular occasions during his time as a junior member that he has long remembered.

One of these occasions was when he was patrolling the streets on a bicycle with other ARP volunteers. He said:

We were suddenly taken aback by the familiar, but always frightening, whistling sound of incendiary bombs falling to the ground. We quickly realised that the banqueting hall of Eltham Palace had been struck, and part of the roof was alight. I, being the youngest and the most agile, was asked to go quickly to the hall and take a hose up to the roof and do what I could to put the fire out. It was extremely frightening, at any moment I could have fallen off the roof or been engulfed by the flames.

However, fortunately the fire did not ravage to a large extent. The Fire Brigade arrived not long after Piers had begun to attack the flames and, together, they extinguished the fire. Piers described it as a 'very useful experience', which also showed him how well the emergency services were working.

Another time, Piers was instructed by the chief ARP warden to stand on guard next to a hole in a road that he suspected had come about following the dropping of an incendiary. Piers' job, with the use of a red hand lamp, was to divert approaching traffic away from the hole (there was little traffic and it was slow moving, so this didn't present a danger). However, although he had his suspicions about what had caused the hole in the road, he had not actually been told. It wasn't until an army truck appeared a few hours later, and after he had successfully diverted a number of cars, that his suspicions were confirmed. On the sides of the truck, in large red letters were the words 'Bomb Disposal'. Upon the arrival of the officer in charge, he was told to 'Buzz off!' as quickly as possible because what they were about to do had the obvious potential of being extremely dangerous. Piers told me he was 'quite affected by the whole experience', knowing that any second the bomb he was guarding could have exploded.

There was no doubt that Piers was very proud to be part of the ARP unit; this was justifiable pride – he was very young to put himself in situations of such danger. He was encouraged in his work with the unit by the resilience of the local people in his community. He spoke to me about a 'keep calm and carry on' mentality. For example, shopkeepers whose livelihoods were potentially destroyed during night-time attacks which caused extensive damage to their property refused to be defeated, often coming out onto the street in the early hours of the following morning, tidying up as much as they could, and putting out large signs saying, 'Open, Business as Usual'. He remembers, too, people laughing as they made 'suitable signs with their fingers, in the direction of Adolf Hitler'.

Within about a week of his eighteenth birthday in March 1942, Piers Alexander de Bernière-Smart was, at last, allowed to sign up for service. He had always wanted to join a cavalry regiment, but he was glad, however, by that time that horses were only used for ceremonial and recreational purposes. After an interview with a recruiting officer he was allocated to the 58th Training Regiment of the Royal Armoured Corps, at Bovington in Dorset. This regiment's specific role was to train young soldiers who were thought to have the potential of becoming officers and senior non-commissioned officers.

He was there for six months, learning the essential skills of armoured fighting, namely gunnery, radio communication, armoured vehicle driving (tanks and all other armoured vehicles, including cars), maintenance and elementary tactics. He then went to the Royal Military College in Sandhurst for six months, finally passing out with a commission later in 1942.

He recalled to me the moment he received his commission, in the presence of his mother and sister, 'to the strains of Auld Lang Syne, I and the other cadets marched up the steps of the fine historic building, following our adjutant, on his old grey charger'. He said he remembered thinking:

> This is it. Now for the reality of war. I was quite overcome by a feeling of pride, tempered by obvious underlying fear of what might lie ahead, whilst being determined at all costs to justify my selection for a commission into the Queen's Bays, one of the oldest regiments in the army and the fourth most senior regiment.

He said he was certain every cadet who passed out with him that day was every bit as proud as he was; all determined to do their utmost for the famous regiment they were about to join. Piers was anxious, too, to remind me that the Bays formed part of the Royal Armoured Corps, a tank division – and that tanks were just as important as cavalry.

Piers' war began with a voyage to Africa – a nine-day journey from Liverpool to Oran. It was a voyage that was as exciting as it was tedious, he recalled, but he feels he should have been more frightened than he actually was, given the last phase of the Battle of the Atlantic had just begun. The Allies were winning by this time, but the threat of German torpedoes was ever present and already they had had an enormous impact, particularly in regard to the Merchant Navy.

In order to minimise the U-boat threat, Piers' ship travelled around the north coast of Ireland, well out into the Atlantic, avoiding the Bay of Biscay, round the Azores and up to Gibraltar in a south-westerly direction. Piers said:

> We only experienced one slightly alarming incident on the way at an early stage when there was a good deal of destroyer activity around us; one destroyer discharged a couple of depth charges over its stern, but we never knew why.

As with so many of the veterans to whom I have been privileged to speak for this book, it is the conversations he remembers most and companionship, jokes and humour. He said:

> I remember standing in the docks at Liverpool, in the shadow of what was clearly a fairly ancient steamer, which one could only study in the very dim lighting. When I went aboard another young officer joined me and we were allocated a cabin and met by our cabin steward who was then a middle-aged, upright, fit looking merchant seaman. He gave us a succinct run down on our general conduct while on board; and a brief history of the ship we were about to set sail in, and in which he had served on for many years. She had been one of the most luxurious vessels on the Liverpool / New York run and had been sold to the Greeks some years before the outbreak of the war. He said she had been hired back from Greece for the duration of the Second World War and converted to a troopship.
>
> The steward was a delightful man, who assessed my travelling companion and me very carefully. He realised that we were high spirited and looking forward to the adventure which held obvious perils, and that he could treat us to a joke or two. When he had finished briefing us – he said, 'Sleep well, don't you worry about torpedoes and all that stuff' and then grinned and said, 'this old girl doesn't need that kind of help to go down.' This typical wartime humour appealed very strongly to both of us.

Piers told me how conscious he was of the divide between conditions for the officers and the troops who slept below – he went below deck every day to talk to them because they were having to cope with hideous travelling conditions, sleeping in hammocks in airless, windowless deck space and only allowed in the open air for a given period each day. By contrast, he and the other officers had above-deck cabins and were able to breathe fresh air whenever they wanted to. He was vastly impressed by the cheerful resilience of the troops below decks, despite their discomfort. Piers said, 'In the process of this journey, one learnt an awful lot. In accordance with the best of British conditions all the troops were well fed and cared for.'

There is one more memory without which Piers' story would not be complete, another enriching memory that he has carried with him throughout his life. It is his story of Christmas, 1944:

> We were bogged down, as were the Germans, in incessant rain as we guarded either side of the River Senio, a fast-flowing river in northern Italy, confined by high flood banks. On Christmas night, by mutual – unspoken – consent we refrained from firing any shots at one another and, instead we sang to each other, all of us bellowing out the words of the famous pop song 'Lilly Marlene'. We sang it first (in English!) and the Germans replied, in German. The damp air felt immeasurably lighter.
>
> Then, somehow or other, bottles of German beer arrived on our side of the river; which we drank, we threw back what little beer we had, and we all sang carols and exchanged friendly greetings.

In among the mud, the rain, the squelchy darkness, they were experiencing perhaps not a season, but moments of true goodwill. Every Christmas, Piers recalls these precious moments. This is a memory of goodwill but also one where both enemy and ally showed the courage to believe they could – at least temporarily – be peaceful with each other. It contrasted with the pain of the memory of the engagement at Montecieco when, after listening to the older officers, he was left with a lasting scepticism about victory leading to long-term peace, and all he could do was play his full part in the smaller battles, so that they did not turn into bigger ones, leading to even more destruction.

These are Piers' foremost wartime memories. However, Piers – again in common with the other veterans whose stories are in this book – has had to dig deep to recall these moments. I hold him in enormous admiration, particularly for telling me about what happened at Coriano Ridge. To recall such painful moments is courageous. To open hearts and minds to me so I can write of these accounts, and in so doing deepen our understanding, is possibly as courageous as many of their actions between 1939 and 1945.

7

CONFETTI – COLIN BELL

Colin was a de Havilland Mosquito pilot. He flew in many very dangerous operations over Germany. This is his story of one especially memorable flight, and also of his training in America.

Colin Bell. (Photo kindly given by Colin Bell)

Skimming rooftops over the heavily defended German capital of Berlin, Flight Lieutenant Colin Bell flew his de Havilland Mosquito as low as possible during the most precarious of all the bombing raids in which he took part towards the end of the Second World War. This was a night-time flight, but it was not dark and certainly not peaceful, for the sky was brightly lit and chaotic with anti-aircraft fire blasting at him from every angle – above, below, starboard, port – every inch of his aircraft was exposed and vulnerable.

Every minute of survival during such a flight, so typical of thousands undertaken by bomber crews throughout the whole of the Second World War, was a gift, and not for a second could Colin, as the pilot, or his navigator, afford to lose concentration. If they flinched for even a moment they could pay the greatest price. On this occasion, their likelihood of survival was further diminished for not only were they under attack from bombs and bullets but radar too. For over half an hour, their Mosquito was vigorously pursued by a German Me 262 fighter aircraft which, at any moment, he said, could have turned them into confetti.

It was an especially frightening and challenging flight because neither Colin, nor his navigator, could actually see the Me 262 that was trying so hard to bring them down. They only knew what was going on because they had detected the fighter on their radar, through a signal represented by a white light on the instrument panel, constantly indicating that an enemy aircraft was trying to close in on them.

It was imperative that the fighter should not obtain clear visual identification of the Mosquito either, and to avoid this Colin had to keep putting his aircraft into a power dive, changing direction to move out of range. This succeeded in the short term, but it was only a matter of minutes before the night fighter, directed by his ground controller, made renewed contact, again through the radar. Repeatedly, Colin had to take evasive action to shake off the Me 262, but, repeatedly, he came back, appearing dangerously close to the Mosquito's tail. This cat-and-mouse activity continued until Colin decided to go down to rooftop level, flying as fast as he could, causing the German fighter to use up a disproportionate amount of fuel.

Colin Bell knew that this type of German jet fighter had only about forty-five minutes' flying time from take-off to return. This was their weakness and, eventually – as Colin and his navigator had hoped so much would be the case – the Me 262 simply could not go on and the chase was abandoned. 'It was all rather nerve-wracking,' Colin said, 'since at any point the German could have overhauled us by 100mph. I don't think he ever did obtain visual contact with us, thankfully – it could have had disastrous results.'

At no other point during the Second World War were Colin's piloting skills and his resolve to return safely to Allied lines so heavily tested. However, his survival on this occasion, as I think he would agree, was in part good fortune.

Our conversation was punctuated with proverbs and sayings which, he told me, guided him not only through the war but throughout his adult life. One of these is a quote from the Italian fourteenth-century philosopher Niccolò Machiavelli, who said, 'Fortune may be the arbiter of one half of our actions, but she still leaves us the other half, or perhaps a little less, to our free will.' Fortune probably did play its part that night, but just a part – surely only a pilot at the top of his game would have been able to cope with the difficulty of flying so low, in such horrendous circumstances.

This was one of fifty Bomber Command raids in which Colin took part, as a guiding aircraft to those with the bombs, such as the Lancasters. However, it was possibly the most memorable, he said. That is not to underestimate the fear and apprehension associated with each and every sortie, and it was entirely justified. The loss of life (and aircraft) for Bomber Command crews in the Second

World War was staggeringly high; over 55,000 men (and some women, ground crew and Air Transport Auxiliary) were killed, out of some 125,000 members, with the majority occurring during operations over Germany.

However, these risky operations had to be undertaken. The German war machine had to be stopped, as Colin repeatedly pointed out, so bombs – in their thousands – had to be dropped to obliterate the threat to the UK and the rest of the world, as it was. The overall target was clear; the war had to be brought to an end, and it had to end in the right way.

In 1942 the British Cabinet, led by Prime Minister Churchill, decreed that 'area bombing' of German cities would be necessary. German transport networks, communication infrastructure and bomb factories had to be destroyed. Their destruction was to come about, in part, through the dropping of bombs and explosives by Bomber Command crews, some in Mosquitos guiding the way for the heavier bomber aircraft, including Lancasters, Halifaxes and Wellingtons.

As Bomber Command undertook its operations releasing their bombs, the loss of civilian life was regrettable but inevitable. Ideally, of course, explosives would have been dropped only on specific targets, but the scale and size of the German war machine made that virtually impossible, so wider-scale attacks were decided upon. Air Chief Marshal Sir Arthur Harris, known as 'Bomber Harris', was in charge of Bomber Command throughout the war, ordered by Churchill to implement the Cabinet policy of 'area bombing'.

Harris duly carried out his orders, beginning with the bombing of Cologne in May 1942. Known as 'Operation Millennium', this was the Royal Air Force's first ever '1,000' bombing raid, during which over 1,000 aircraft dropped over 2,000 tonnes of explosives, killing around 470 people and leaving hundreds homeless but, crucially, also resulted in the destruction of some forty factories.

It was hoped that the scale of this attack alone might intimidate German leaders enough to bring about the beginning of the end of the war. But there wasn't enough of a dent to German morale on this occasion and it was quickly realised by Harris and the British politicians that more attacks would be needed as the war against the Allies on battlefields across Europe and the world was intensifying, alongside the suffering being inflicted on thousands of prisoners held in German concentration camps.

Germany, during the Second World War, was, as Colin reminded me, unrelenting in its determination to rule – whatever the cost. It was domination for domination's sake, with the Nazis becoming extremely bitter following the outcome of the First World War, and Germany's subsequent humiliation regarding the Treaty of Versailles.

This treaty angered the Germans greatly, particularly because Germany was not invited to take part in the negotiations. It had signed the Armistice in 1918 and was ordered to sign the treaty in June the following year. Germany was also angry that it was being forced to accept some of the blame for bringing about the First World War. Germany's view was that it was a necessary evil in order to defend itself against Russia, which had mobilised in July 1914 with Great Britain and France against the Ottoman Empire, which was siding with Germany.

The Treaty of Versailles had massive, long-lasting consequences for Germany. It prohibited the country from rebuilding its defences, not even allowing it to position many troops in the country itself. Germany was also heavily financially penalised and forced to surrender much of its land, with huge parts of it given to France and Poland. Neither was it allowed to unite with Austria.

Germany spent much of the intervening war years planning how to recover and rebuild. By the time the Second World War came around, it had developed an enormous infrastructure and weaponry, becoming ruthless and determined to be the nation it wanted to be. It had, as Colin pointed out, in addition to the military might of the *Wehrmacht* – its armed forces, combining the Luftwaffe (air force), Kriegsmarine (navy) and the Heer (army) – it had developed and was continuing to develop a range of rockets, known as 'V' weapons. There were three versions of V rocket (*Vergeltungswaffen* in German) – I, II and III – which were essentially long-range artillery rockets specifically designed for strategic bombing in Europe.

The V-2, known as Hitler's 'vengeance' rocket, was one of world's first ballistic missiles and was a particularly frightening weapon of mass destruction. Once released, this 13-tonne missile would fly at over 3,000mph, hurtling towards its targets without mercy. Death probably came very quickly and any survivors would have had fearful earache following massive sonic booms that came after landing.

August 1944 was an especially terrible month for London because of the V-2. Hundreds of lives were lost in over 500 direct strikes.

Colin told me that part of Bomber Command's defensive operation was to attack the sites where these rockets were being developed, particularly in the location of Peenemünde, a scientific and manufacturing site on an island in the Baltic Sea. Thousands of Royal Air Force heavy bombers dropped hundreds of tons of explosives here during four huge raids, in an operation known as 'Operation Hydra', which resulted in severe damage to laboratories, testing sites and equipment.

However, while these sites were unarguably legitimate targets, the 'area bombing' of German cities has, since the end of the war, drawn much criticism, with Bomber Command, unfairly in Colin's view, blamed for the killing of civilians, even though it was acting under instruction, carrying out its duties gallantly and courageously (and in doing so, facing phenomenal risk) to bring down the enemy. Colin is emphatic that the whole of Bomber Command's activity was justifiable because it was entirely in defence of this country. 'We did what we had to do,' he said, 'for our men, our women and our children.' He remains an unequivocally proud member of this command, which had the highest casualty rate of all units in the Second World War; only the infantry in the trenches in the First World War matched their rate of attrition.

Drawing my attention to other cities which came under attack during the 'area bombing' campaign, including Hamburg in 1943 (which caused the deaths of approximately 35,000 and permanent damage to factories), Dresden and Berlin (the fall of which, in May 1945, led to the end of the war, Hitler himself not even witnessing it because he committed suicide on 30 April), Colin acknowledged the appalling nature of these attacks. However, regarding Dresden in February 1945 (which resulted in the deaths of over 25,000), he said:

> We simply did what we had to do. Dresden was a highly developed centre for war production, and an essential rail centre through which 20,000 troops passed each and every day. It was a legitimate target for Bomber Command, contrary to the views of ill-informed people of the current generation.

Colin showed me the words of a speech that he has framed and hung in the hallway of his home. In 1942, the German Minister of Agriculture articulated the Nazi aim with the following spine-chilling words:

> As soon as we beat England, we shall make an end of you Englishmen, once and for all. Able-bodied men and women will be exported as slaves to the continent. The old and the weak will be exterminated. All men remaining in Britain as slaves will be sterilised: a million or two of the young women of the

Nordic type will be segregated in a number of stud farms where, with the assistance of picked German sires, during a period of 12 years, they will produce annually a series of Nordic infants to be brought up in every way as Germans. These infants will form the future population of Britain … thus in a generation or two, the British will disappear.

★★★

Colin Bell joined 608 Squadron in 1944 – inevitably apprehensive but also excited, not least because 608 flew Mosquitos, in what was known as the Night Light Striking Force of Bomber Command. Flying 1,726 sorties during 246 bombing raids, 608 Squadron amazingly only suffered the loss of nine Mosquitos. Out of all of the Second World War aircraft, Colin said this was the one – if he had had the choice – he would have chosen to fly. It was nicknamed the 'Wooden Wonder', and he had nothing but praise for this relatively small machine, constructed partly of wood, which resulted in it being the lightest and fastest of all the Second World War aircraft. I expressed surprise at this – I would have thought that being in a wooden aeroplane would have been the most terrifying because it would be the quickest to go up in flames if it was hit, but Colin told me precisely to the contrary. 'Knowing you were in a machine that could pull away from any German fighter, other than a jet, was fantastic,' he said.

Designed and constructed by Geoffrey de Havilland, who proved himself to be a world leader in aviation development during the years between the wars, there was little to rival the Mosquito when it first entered service in late 1941 as an unarmed, high-speed, high-altitude reconnaissance aircraft. It was extremely versatile. 'Not many other aircraft took on so many "jobs",' Colin said. As the war progressed, it was used during the day and night as a fighter and bomber and a U-boat hunter, in addition to its principal role of being a pathfinder aircraft, involving the release of flares for heavier bombers to indicate the whereabouts of their targets.

Colin told me that one of the main reasons he was more than content to be a Mosquito pilot was because the Germans really 'hated it'. Its unique design 'confounded the Huns', he said, laughing as he recalled the frustration of the Nazi leader Hermann Göring, who declared:

> In 1940 I could fly as far as Glasgow in most of my aircraft, but not now. It makes me furious when I see the Mosquito. I turn green and yellow with envy. The British, who can afford aluminium better than we can, knock together a beautiful wooden aircraft that every piano factory is building … they have the geniuses and we have the nincompoops.

Colin Bell was 19 years old when he applied to join the Royal Air Force. He was not accepted immediately, but he persevered, and the following year was taken on as a volunteer. In 1941 he was fully signed up and went to America for training. His first posting was to Lakeland in Florida, where he was taught to fly on a Boeing Stearman, which he described as a speedy and tremendously 'good fun' bi-plane trainer aircraft. After leaving Florida, Colin went to Georgia in the south-east of America to develop his skills on a Vultee, another single-engine plane, but larger, faster and not a bi-plane. After mastering the Vultee, Colin went to Alabama to complete his training on a AT-6 Harvard trainer.

Colin finally received his American wings in late 1941 and was looking forward to returning to the UK so, at last, he said, he 'could get on with the job'. However, Colin's plans were thrown into complete disarray by one of the most catastrophic events in the history of the Second World War. As he was preparing to leave Alabama, the Japanese Imperial Navy Air Service was preparing the carnage it was about to unleash at Pearl Harbor, in

Hawaii. In the early hours (US time) of 7 December 1941, over 350 Japanese aircraft brought down 188 American aircraft and sank four battleships, killing over 2,400 Americans and wounding around 1,700.

It was, said President Roosevelt, 'a date that will live in Infamy'. The Americans were furious and had been taken completely by surprise. Diplomatic efforts for peace in the Pacific region, although difficult, were still underway and war had not been declared.

It was not long before President Roosevelt took a firm stand and responded by declaring war on Japan. Colin, although stunned by the scale of the attack and horrified by the number of casualties, felt an inner sense of calm after hearing news of the Pearl Harbor bombing and the American reaction. He felt certain that it would now only be a matter of time before America would declare support for the Allies, which would hasten the end of the war. Because of Pearl Harbor, he was certain that victory for the Allies was around the corner. It became a matter of 'when', not 'if'.

Winston Churchill, too, confirmed that Colin's thoughts were not misplaced. Colin was able to tune into the prime minister's address to the British people during which he asserted Britain's unflinching support for America, and also his concerns about the havoc Japan was also unleashing in the Far East. It was later reported that although Churchill was undoubtedly horrified by the conduct of the Japanese in Pearl Harbor, the night he heard what had happened, 'he slept the sleep of the saved and the thankful'.

Colin Bell's wartime service then took an unexpected course. Instead of returning to Europe and taking up duties in combat, it was a role reversal. Suddenly, hundreds of young American cadets were recruited to join the war effort and Colin was required to stay in the USA to train a number of them. He was instructed to return to the Advanced Training Corps field in Alabama to take up his teaching role.

'It was like the blind leading the blind,' he told me, with his wonderful sense of humour coming to the fore. The most amusing thing about it all, he said, was that most of the cadets were 'huge – they were all about six feet tall, weighing 14 stone, and I was just five feet, six inches and just over half their weight'. Colin described them as 'excellent' chaps: diligent, good humoured and hardworking. He had the utmost respect for them. Trainers and cadets alike all did their best to hone the skills required as quickly as possible so as to get to work and bring about the end of the war.

It was while in America that Colin had an 'awakening' of another kind, a realisation of a course of action that was to shape the rest of his life. Before going to America for training, he had met Kathlyn and had fallen determinedly and passionately in love. But, his pursuit of her was fraught with difficulty. When he met her, he said, she was 'not in the least bit interested' in him, and he was about to be posted abroad.

However, Colin decided to take his chances, writing to her and, eventually, while still in America, he was thrilled to receive a letter back. He shared the correspondence with his roommate, a close friend and confidante called Ken Arrowsmith who simply responded by saying, 'Marry her'.

That is exactly what he did. Colin married Kathlyn in July 1943 and they honeymooned for three days in Windsor. The first of their two children, a daughter, was born in September 1944.

Sadly, Colin was widowed in December 2016 after seventy-three years of marriage.

As with the war, he told me how he and Kathlyn worked through everything, overcoming life's obstacles with a sense of humour that enabled them to put everything that happened into perspective. After all, he said, taken from the musical *Cabaret*, which he loves, 'Life is a cabaret, old chum! Come to the cabaret!'

Colin knows that one day, his cabaret will be over (he asked me to write that!). He has often spoken publicly during the post-war years about his pride in the role he played during the war, giving thanks for what he has, and for the life lessons it taught him. However – and he specifically asked me to write this, too – he looks forward, with peace, to rejoining the love of his life …

8

CREATIVITY IS GOOD FOR THE SOUL – MADY GERRARD

A Hungarian Jew, in her early teens Mady was sent to Auschwitz and Bergen-Belsen. These are her memories of those days, her release, and the life she made for herself afterwards.

Mady Gerrard. (Photo kindly given by Mady Gerrard)

'I can't see her face, I just can't remember what she looked like, they took my photographs away.' Hungarian-born Mady Gerrard was talking to me about her Great Aunt Gisella, who became a mother to her after her fifth birthday. Her birth mother was ill with tuberculosis during her infant years and died when Mady was 7. Because her parents had divorced, her father was not around to care for her and, just before Christmas in 1935, the duty of care for Mady fell to Gisella, affectionately known to her as Aunt Gisi, and her equally kind husband, Uncle Joseph.

Mady lived with them for the following nine years in the city of Keszthely, a thriving market town in the west of Hungary. Overlooked by forests and hills on one side and touching the shores of Lake Balaton – one of central Europe's largest lakes – on the other, Keszthely couldn't have been more beautifully situated, and the formative childhood years Mady spent there were happy ones, for which she has long been grateful:

> I learnt so much from my little great aunt. She taught me eve-rything. She was so good to me – my mother wouldn't have been any better. And yet I haven't got a photograph of her, or my uncle, in my possession, and it doesn't matter what I do, I can't remember their faces. Taking my photographs of them away from me is something I will never be able to forgive the Germans for. Why they had to do that … I don't know, what was the point of taking our photographs away?

Mady answered these rhetorical questions herself, shaking her head with a resentment she has carried through her life, 'It was just to punish us, I suppose.' She didn't say it, but she knew. Her crime – in the eyes of the Germans – was that she was a Jew. The photographs Mady had of Aunt Gisella and Uncle Joseph were taken from her shortly after they were killed at Auschwitz in 1944.

This was my introduction, by Mady, to her memories of being a childhood prisoner, first of all at Auschwitz and then Bergen-Belsen. However, in stark contrast to the grey bleakness of the Holocaust, in telling me about Aunt Gisi, she also introduced me to her love of colour and the joy that bright colours have given her throughout her life – colours in wool and fabric that her Aunt Gisi taught her about in the peaceful years before her mind was forever tainted by the horror of the Holocaust.

Mady Gerrard was liberated from the Bergen-Belsen concentration camp, in northern Germany, at the age of 15. Of the 60,000 men, women and children incarcerated, she was one of less than 10,000 to come out alive. When we met, Mady had just had her eighty-eighth birthday. I interviewed her in the kitchen of her cosy, colourful home in south Wales, which was bursting with cards and flowers, reflecting the life in colour she has created for herself. Inspired by Aunt Gisi, in the post-war years she established a fashion design label, simply known as Mady Gerrard, crocheting and creating silk haute couture designer clothes and accessories, in beautiful colours (except blue – the reason for which will be told later). Her success with Mady Gerrard has been phenomenal; it is a wonderful tribute to her aunt, who was her inspiration, teaching Mady the skills she needed from the workshop she ran in Keszthely.

When she was liberated from Belsen in April 1945, Mady was physically extremely weak (weighing just 24kg) and – almost needless to say – very deeply traumatised. But she was not defeated. At the time, with the Holocaust, the Germans set out to do their utmost to eliminate the Jews, and even those they did not kill they wanted to hurt as much as they could by torturing them emotionally, leaving them with mental scars that would never heal.

Mady has undoubtedly lived with emotional wounds throughout her life, probably more painful than most of us will ever comprehend, even during our darkest moments. However, in spite of her very fragile state, Mady emerged from the agony of her experience with a strength and determination that sets the bar very high on what can be achieved with courage and being practical – an amazingly strong work ethic.

Mady's experience reveals the very worst of humanity. The Holocaust exposes the horrible, inescapable fact that if humankind is willing, it can be utterly despicable. Evil is too shallow a word for the cruelty and deprivation inflicted upon other human beings by those with minds so warped and vile they perpetuated this misery, without compassion, day after day. But in contrast, Mady herself reveals the very best of humanity. She has married, is a mother, and established a successful business, the products of which have been highly sought after.

The Second World War Holocaust is without doubt one of the most hideous episodes of human history, but of course it is not unique. Even to this day, as I write, somewhere in the world deliberate pain will be being inflicted. A precious life will be ending and a heart subsequently being broken. However, almost all of us (thankfully) only really know of this chaos and destruction because we read of it in newspapers and hear about it on television and radio. Even in our bleakest moments, and I think this will be the case for most of the readers of this book, our darkness is punctuated with some light, even if at times that light is only a tiny chink.

I think at this point I need to admit how difficult I am finding it to write this chapter because, in order to give it justice, I need somehow to at least begin to appreciate the level of suffering Mady experienced, and I simply can't do that. The torture inflicted at the camps was so relentless it seemed to be limitless. There was nothing the Nazis wouldn't do, such was their determination to destroy the Jewish race, and so entrenched was their belief that they were racially superior to the Jews that those 'under' them should be destroyed. So now that Mady has read this chapter, I am especially grateful to her for allowing me to publish it. This account is so vital.

Most of us have a vague idea what the Holocaust was, from reading about it and seeing photographs of what happened in its midst, during which the Nazis murdered some 6 million European Jews as part of their systematic plan of mass genocide. However, in writing of the agonies inflicted on the thousands so unfortunate to be held captive at the camps the Nazis established to inflict the pain, it is necessary to think about those who unleashed the suffering. Because, day after day, for more than twelve years, beginning in 1933 with Adolf Hitler's appointment as Chancellor of Germany, hundreds of compliant Nazis attempted to overwhelm and suffocate the Jewish people by whatever means they could.

So we must, I think, consider what drove the Nazis to inflict such pain and how they could behave in the way they did at the many camps they established throughout Germany and occupied Poland. As I write, I am trying to empathise (in my limited way) with the physical and emotional pain Mady experienced, while trying to get to grips with those who perpetrated the suffering. That is actually even harder. In thinking, reading and writing about the Holocaust there is simply no escaping at all the fact that human beings, if they choose to, are capable of utterly despicable, depraved behaviour.

I am not really succeeding here in my quest to even begin to understand how a human being can be as unstintingly cruel as they were in the Holocaust. This is not supposed to be a detailed exploration of the human mind; I am not a psychologist. However, I suppose I wouldn't be writing this if I wasn't interested or didn't care about what motivates and drives human beings to do what they do. Surely no one – not even those so brainwashed as the Nazis in their hatred of the Jews between 1933 and 1945 – could do what they did without even a scrap of feeling or regret about what they were doing.

I had to ask Mady, therefore, if she ever felt that those conducting such vile actions found it hard to do so. She was not at all unkind in her reply, but brutally honest, and I was left feeling rather naïve and despondent. 'None at all,' she said quickly. 'Don't you understand? They wanted us to die. They wanted us all to die.' I asked her this question after she had told me how she was paraded, while at Bergen-Belsen, day after day with other girls of her age, in front of the guards, during which they would be told to go in either of two directions. One direction would lead them back to incarceration, the other would be to a death chamber.

So Mady's story is very important. Because the Holocaust did happen, and because these camps did exist and did result in so much agony and loss of life, it is very important that it is remembered, and the pain of those who experienced it is acknowledged. And, as much as facts, figures and historical documents tell the story, if you – the reader – truly want to comprehend not just the scale of the suffering but the wretchedness of it, personal testimonies are essential. In opening her heart to me, Mady is giving remembrance to so many who quite simply never had the opportunity to do so themselves. They must never be forgotten.

It was in March 1944, at the tender age of 14, that Mady was sent to Auschwitz, together with her aunt and uncle and hundreds of other residents of Keszthely. Prior to their being forced out of their home, German forces had entered the town, replacing peace with fear and dread. It was the same throughout the rest of Hungary. There was little the Jewish people could do in the face of the strength of Germany, making the people scapegoats for political decisions taken by Hungarian leaders throughout the war of which, of course, they had not been a part.

Mady spoke first about Auschwitz and her later liberation from the Bergen-Belsen concentration camp, which she has described as actually even worse. About her time at Auschwitz, she has written that it taught her that the word 'awful' had degrees. She wrote:

The food was 'awful', but in Belsen it was 'most awful'. We existed from the end of January until the middle of April somehow and the last two to three weeks were even more than 'most awful'. We were given some hot liquid and that was all. People were dropping dead by the minute and I don't remember any sort of sanitation or ever having a bath or shower in Belsen.

Mady described Auschwitz as an almost perfect 'killing machine', but Belsen:

> … having been deserted by the high officers and left to its misery, disease and infestations, was the hell that nightmares are made of and the cruelty was almost incomprehensible to most of mankind.

Mady wrote of her conviction that people suffered with 'brain-cell destruction' due to starvation, and of piles of stinking, dirty naked bodies that would occasionally 'move' if a body was thrown onto it that was not quite dead.

Auschwitz, she recalled, was like a ghost town – it had the words *'ARBEIT MACHT FREI'* ('WORK MAKES FREE') engraved above its gates. These words, Mady says, have been carved on her mind forever:

> Every night, open lorries filled with hundreds of innocent, tragic victims were driven to the gas chambers. Some were screaming, some were crying, but the lorries rolled on as part of the well-oiled death machine of the Third Reich. Gassing people only took two minutes. Sometimes we wondered how the dead bodies were removed to the crematoria and then we started to hear about the *Sonderkommandos*, who were the special groups of men whose job it was to remove the bodies. This horror cannot be imagined by normal human beings – one had to be there.

The *Sonderkommandos* were selected exclusively from professional people, including doctors, solicitors, chemists and archaeologists. The Germans were real perfectionists and employed highly qualified groups of intellectuals to transfer dead bodies from the gas chambers into the furnaces. It may have been yet another means of humiliation for the Jews, but whoever they used for cleaning up the mess that mass murder leaves in its wake, Auschwitz was well organised, and no bodies were left around. Auschwitz was clean and tidy: we didn't even have lice.

In contrast to the almost eerie 'cleanliness' of Auschwitz, the filth and depravity of Bergen-Belsen was laid bare later at the trials of those responsible, held at the British Military Court in Luneburg. Brigadier Glyn Hughes, one of the main witnesses for the prosecution observed:

Shortly before the 15th April 1945, German officers came to the headquarters of 8th Corps and asked for a truce in respect of the Belsen camp, after it had been captured. There were piles of corpses lying all over the camp. Even within the huts there were numbers of bodies, some even in the same bunks as the living. Most of the internees were suffering from some form of gastro-enteritis and were too weak to leave. The lavatories in the huts had long been out of use. Those who were strong enough could get into the appropriate compounds, but others performed their natural actions from where they were. The compounds were a mass of human excreta.

Some of the huts had bunks, but not many, and they were filled absolutely to overflowing with prisoners in every stage of emaciation and disease. There was not room for them to lie down at full length in the huts. In the most crowded there were anything from 600 to 1,000 people in accommodation which should have taken 100. The principal causes of death in Belsen were lack of food and washing facilities which led to lice and the spread of typhus. Even after liberation matters were not easy in the way of food, in spite of the facilities the British had, because special feeding was necessary.

The above describes the bigger picture but then there are the individuals. The accumulation of cruelty at Bergen-Belsen included the piling up of rotten corpses, each one a person who lay next to another, resulting in a mass of decomposition and becoming one mass of stinking flesh. Each body, each person, had they survived, would have had their own story, and each one's passing in that appalling way would have left someone behind who loved them. That is why Mady's story matters so much.

The pain, the grief, the horror in itself is a story, but it also has to be written about in the context of thinking how it is possible for human beings to be brainwashed into such depraved behaviour. We know what they wanted to do – the Germans wanted rid of the Jewish people. But this? The more I write and learn about it, the more it surpasses understanding.

Mady has written and spoken to me particularly about a man called Dr Mengele – known to the inmates at the time as the 'Angel of Death'. He was one of the principal guards who would watch her and the other young girls as he forced them to file, naked, past him, day after day. She said:

I couldn't help but wonder if he had sexual fantasies as he watched us. Some of the girls were beautiful, at least in the first few weeks before they became skeletons – they must have looked interesting to any man. We didn't find out if Mengele took part in the rape sessions that many of the German guards were involved in, but with his power he could have amused himself in any way he wished, privately or otherwise. The guards drank and raped the inmates at will – it was part of their normal behaviour and it was recreation for them.

There was, however, another German guard who always wore a blue shirt. It was this person who has given Mady a lifelong aversion to the colour blue. This guard was a woman who, Mady told me, possibly made her psychopathic conduct even harder to accept – 'because she was a woman, her cruelty was unexpected'. As Mengele was the 'Angel of Death', she – Irma Grese – was known as the 'Queen of Death'. Mady described her as 'blonde, blue-eyed and deadly, striking in appearance and she had a leather thong whip protruding from [her] right leather boot'. She said:

> We never knew when she would turn up and when she did would never hesitate to use her whip on some helpless person who had unwittingly annoyed her, and then she would beat them until they were dead.
>
> We had all watched her abuse those poor people. They were powerless and submissive as she stood over them. She showed no mercy and flogged them with a detached expression on her face as though she was performing any normal household chore. We who were terrified stood in silence – paralysed with fright in case we were the next victim.

If Irma Grese did have any sick satisfaction for what she did at Bergen-Belsen it did not last for long; she was one of thirty German officers sentenced to death by hanging during the trial at the British Military Court in Luneburg, in September 1945. During the hearing, testimonies from survivors provided details of the acts of sadism, beatings and arbitrary shootings she inflicted, in addition to accounts of her unleashing her half-starved aggressive dogs upon the emaciated inmates. It has also been documented that she had lampshades made of human skin in her hut.

At the beginning of the war, Hungary was aligned to Germany in its battle against Russia; a coalition which afforded Hungarian Jews a degree of protection almost unparalleled in the rest of Europe. However, at the same time the Prime Minister of Hungary, Miklos Kallay, was also in talks with Britain and America, suggesting that Hungary was open to 'switching sides' if the Allies were able to reach its border. These discussions amounted to the betrayal for which Germany decided to punish Hungary, hence the occupation and the subsequent murder – mostly through delivery to gas chambers – of over 550,000 Hungarian Jews in the Holocaust.

It was in March 1944 that the beating heart of Keszthely was torn out. For years that followed, it was a shadow of its former self, suffering a collective grief from which no one had been able to escape. Mady returned to Hungary after the war, but to a completely different country. 'No one,' she said, 'escaped the impact of German occupation during the war, and the Russian occupation afterwards. Everybody was changed by it.'

She recalled, for example, the sadness of the father of one her best friends – a girl called Lilly – who had not escaped death while they were together at Bergen-Belsen. She told me how she and Lilly had been forced to parade in front of the SS guards one evening at Belsen, after which they were given their instructions as to what to do next, through a gesture of the guard's hand. This gesture, Mady said:

> … would indicate whether we should take the right hand queue or the left, which meant nothing to him, but life or death for us. We were both gestured to the 'infirmary', which meant the gas chamber. I escaped by climbing over a door, but Lilly didn't come with me and I never saw her again.
>
> This must have been the worst day of my life, it took me more than 30 years to forgive myself, I kept on blaming myself.

Mady visited Lilly's father during the very difficult post-war years. However, it was not a reunion that she recalled brought either of them any comfort. Prior to the war, she said, he was a clever, articulate, kind man, but because of Auschwitz, 'he lost his mind', 'not only did he lose Lilly, but he also lost his other daughter and his first wife'. He did marry again, said Mady, but eventually committed suicide after his second wife died of cancer. Mady said, 'He asked me why I didn't have the decency to let Lilly come home, instead of me. What could I say? I had nobody to come back for, yet I came home. Lilly didn't.'

The seeds of destruction of Keszthely, implanted so firmly by the Germans in 1944, went on during this time to be watered, sadly, by its own people after the war with pillaging and looting by locals who had been left with very little. Mady wrote:

> Everything was removed for souvenirs or more likely for firewood and, if the war-stricken people were so poor and so desperate for firewood during that extremely difficult period, who can blame them for taking what they needed? Everything good and worth-while in Keszthely was ruined – even the beautiful palace of Prince Feistetich – with penknives people cut pieces out of the exquisite handmade tapestries, and they defecated on the beautiful chairs that had been so carefully carved by craftsmen and stole everything that was moveable – even the old wood-block floors that had been made years before were destroyed.

Mady returned to Hungary after the war in 1946; she stayed for ten years. It was during this time that she began to build up her business. But it was not a happy time for her – far from it. She wrote:

> Eastern Europe looked very sad the year after the war ended. The people were downtrodden, they were badly dressed

and poor; buildings had been destroyed and food was far from plentiful.

She had spent time in Sweden between the end of the war and her return to Hungary, cared for by a delegation from the Swedish Red Cross. She described her journey to Scandinavia as an 'unreal dream after experiencing a grotesque nightmare'. She saw the northern lights and was fed and cared for so diligently by the staff that within seven weeks she more than doubled in weight, going from 25 to 60kg. 'I was chubby!' she said, 'But better to be chubby and alive, than skinny and dead.'

But Sweden was not somewhere she belonged forever; she was taken there to recover, at least physically, which she did. So from there, she returned to Hungary – nervous about how she might find her homeland but unprepared for the awfulness of what she did find. She went there, principally, in search of so many people she had loved, but she found virtually no one. After Sweden, she said, being in Hungary was like 'giving up a heaven for another hell'.

It was also during these post-war years in Hungary in 1953 that Mady met and married her first husband and then gave birth to her daughter – a little girl they name Ildiko. However, the marriage did not last and within two years she and her husband separated. Mady worked harder than ever. It was during this time that she learnt to design knitwear and use a knitting machine, and after Ildiko (Ildi for short) was born, she nursed her child on her 'left arm and controlled the knitting machine with my right'.

However, as hard as it was being back in Hungary, Mady knew she was lucky to be alive. 'I didn't have a licence to stay alive,' she said. Her only way of explaining the fact she came out of Belsen alive was luck. 'I was one who was lucky, I suppose,' she said. 'Most were unlucky.'

The war might have finished, but the legacy it left in Hungary was dreadful. The Russians, under Stalin, had occupied the country since the end of the war and its people, already demoralised by the legacy of the Holocaust, then suffered the indignity of being ruled by a controlling Communist regime that impinged upon their liberty and repressed their spirits. The Russians intimidated the Hungarians with the might of their military. Guards and tanks patrolled the streets, threatening (and inflicting) torture and punishment on those who dared oppose the regime.

Joseph Stalin died in 1953, which led to an air of rebellion beginning to perpetuate and three years later, in October 1956, the Revolution (or Uprising) began. It lasted for around three weeks; the Hungarian people had simply had enough. However, it started as it ended – in defeat. Students in Budapest were some of the first to take to the streets, however, they were quickly brought down by Russian police, who fired at them and killed the student who launched the revolution by wrapping himself in the Hungarian national flag and allowing his friends to hold him up high, as a symbol of the freedom many were so longing for.

The student was the first of over 2,500 Hungarians who were killed during the Uprising, in addition to 700 Russians who died. Over 200,000 of the locals fled as refugees, many of whom went to Austria. Mady and Ildi were two of them.

But even their journey to Austria was challenging, exhausting and unpredictable, involving a 14-mile walk in cold, wet autumn weather, with the constant threat of being captured by the Russians at any moment. That said, in spite of the uncertainty, this walk marked the beginning of a wonderful new chapter for Mady and Ildi. Their stay in Austria was short, and within five weeks of leaving Hungary, Mady decided she wanted to cross the Channel and come to the United Kingdom. They found a home in Wales, receiving, she recalled, the warmest of welcomes from the Welsh in Cardiff.

Mady and Ildi were happy there, for a while. Mady began to build up her business, knitting and crocheting, and delighting in the joy and comfort she was able to give those who bought her lovingly made clothes. By 1959, she had managed to buy her own home, renting out a couple of rooms to lodgers who helped her pay the mortgage for her house and small shop. Mady beavered away, championing the hard work ethic instilled in her by Aunt Gisi and establishing an unparalleled reputation, which eventually took her away from Wales to North America. In 1964 she crossed the Atlantic, arriving first in Toronto, then on to New York.

It took time for her to settle in New York. As has been the story of Mady's life, she began with little but believed in herself and what she could do and worked as hard as she could. At the beginning of her life there, she lived in a small room in a hotel with cockroaches. By the end of her fourteen years, she was able to list the singer Dionne Warwick among her clients, as well as Presidential First Ladies, Nancy Regan and Pat Nixon.

Mady showed me photographs, telling the story of her amazing designer journey, and I felt proud to be shown around the workshop of her cosy cottage, which was bursting with soft, bright, cheerful baby blankets and rails of silk jackets and shirts. 'Being creative,' she said, 'is good for the soul.'

And even in Bergen-Belsen, from where she was liberated almost exactly seventy-three years before my visit, she found an outlet for her creativity, an outlet that brought comfort and joy — and colour — among the bleakness that had become her life. She and some of the other young girls were given some work to do sorting out thin electrical wires:

Our job was to pull out the wire from the coloured outside cover, and the covers were made of small beads. The beads were perfect for necklaces, so we started to make some and gave them to the German ladies in charge of us, who were really pleased with them. They gave us some extra bread and margarine, in exchange for the little necklaces. After all they didn't have much either, so it worked for everyone.

So it was, among these delicate little necklaces, that she was able to give a little bit of happiness to those making them and to those who received them. But even as she did so, she had no idea what lay ahead, not knowing if each day could be her last.

But, of course, she was spared and was liberated from Bergen-Belsen on 15 April 1945. She was discovered, emaciated, bald and despairing among the filthy stench of death that was Bergen-Belsen by Lieutenant John Randall, then a 24-year-old member of the SAS. It was during a reconnaissance mission in the part of Germany where Bergen-Belsen was situated that he came across the camp and he was the first Allied soldier to enter. Totally unprepared for what he found, and in deep shock, he began the process of liberating the prisoners from the hell they were in, meeting no resistance from the guards, who by then knew the war was lost and were certain, probably, that they were going to face justice. They were right.

It was John Randall who gave Mady back her life. In an article for the *Daily Telegraph* on 15 April 2005, printed to mark the sixtieth anniversary of the liberation of prisoners from Bergen-Belsen, Randall was one of those interviewed. He has since died, but in the article, he said:

We just drove through the gates [of the camp] because they were open. There were one or two totally dejected-looking guards, but they made no effort to shoot. They didn't even stop us. About 30 yards into the camp, my Jeep was suddenly surrounded by a group of around 100 emaciated prisoners. Most of them were in black-and-white striped prison uniforms and the rest wore a terrible assortment of ragged clothes. It was the state of these inmates that made me realise this was no ordinary POW camp. As to its name or place I had no idea.

He went on to mention that some 15-year-old 'almost skeletons' approached him and said they only had a 'few days to live and no hope', but his arrival gave them hope. Mady was one of the 'skeletons'. He rescued her …

That could be the end of this story. But it isn't. Mady saw the article, and John Randall – then 85 years old – came back into her life. The article was accompanied by a photograph and she described her excitement to me upon seeing it – absolute joy. It was one of those clearly defining moments of life which she will long remember. She told me she was with only her dog, in her kitchen and so it was with him that she first shared her profound thrill. The article led to much happiness for her. Through the *Daily Telegraph* she was reunited with him and there began a profound and special friendship, between not only the two of them but also their families.

It would be almost impossible for anyone, even a member of the SAS who had been through the war as John Randall had, not to be affected by what they saw upon going through the gates of Bergen-Belsen. And he was affected, deeply troubled, but stirred into action, as a result saving lives. He wrote the foreword in Mady's book *Full Circle*, in which he wrote:

> The attempted annihilation of the Jewish people and the manner of its execution must always remain one of the greatest and most disgraceful crimes in history. The thousands of brilliantly talented people from all aspects of our lives – art, literature, medicine, music, philosophy - and every walk of life is so awful that its magnitude can never be exaggerated.

In spite of the horrors the survivors have a history of extraordinary bravery, a determination to survive and the indomitable spirit to never give up hope. This must be an inspiration to all of us.

And he is right. If we can draw any good at all from the dreadful pain and loss of the Holocaust it must be the inspiration of strength from those who survived and went on to lead good and fulfilling lives afterwards, such as Mady. In a personal note to her, John Randall wrote:

> With the war over but still no security living in an ugly world still full of hate and depravity – there is still hope and determination to survive. Finally, bit by bit, survival and success – you have fought and won.
>
> Congratulations – I am proud to know you and I am lucky to have played a tiny part in your survival.

Mady Gerrard certainly has an appreciation of life that is inspiring; yet another reason why her story is important. After living through the Holocaust, I doubt she has ever taken a single day for granted. What she has achieved is an example to us all. I have written it earlier, but I will do so again – her story matters so much, we can and must learn from her strength and example. She said:

> I am fortunate because I came out of that hell extremely well. I am almost healthy, and I don't cry when someone questions me about Auschwitz and the war. Even though there are things that would reveal to an analyst the underlying torments that lie deep within me, I can laugh, and I feel that life is very important to me.

John Randall, however, summed up the importance of devoting full remembrance to this appalling episode, in a way that gives it purpose and almost a reason. He wrote:

> My final sobering fear is that these crimes are already happening again, and we must all resolve to fight this situation as vigorously as we can.

9

'THET LUK LOIKE A GRET OL' PIG' – PETER BLACKBURN

Peter was in the Home Guard in Norfolk. He was at school when the war began. This story tells of the important work the Home Guard did 'behind the front lines', and of other important accounts he gathered from local people when they returned after 1945.

Peter Blackburn. (Photo kindly given by Alison Schwier)

'Agh, Ouch!' laughed Peter Blackburn, recalling the stinging pain of a caning he received seventy years ago, when he was just 14 years old. Yet, in spite of the pain, the punishment was not one he regretted receiving, such was the reason for which the birch had met his backside. His reprimand – also administered to around thirty of his peers – was for venturing beyond the borders of his prep school near Bury St Edmunds in Suffolk to examine the remains of a German Junkers Ju 88 aeroplane that had been shot down during a skirmish with a Spitfire and a Hurricane.

The Second World War became real for Peter when he first saw the Ju 88 circling over his school. He said:

We stood there, watching it, and as we did so it began to turn. The pilot must have seen the large house (that was our school building); for safety we all ran inside pretty quick and immediately the air raid siren went, and everybody rushed down to the cellars, so we didn't actually see what happened.

But we learned afterwards, the German had used his bombs elsewhere, but he machine-gunned the house, and most of the bullets went into the headmaster's study. Anyway, Allied planes appeared and shot him down, and he landed the other side of the lake. This lake went right through the grounds of our school and we used to go fishing there, and sometimes walk along the bank. However, we weren't allowed to go across the other side, over the bridge, without special permission. But we did, and we liked it because there was a lot of wildlife, a tremendous variety of birds, because much of the lake had reeds and there were warblers and all other types of birds, coots, water hens. We'd enjoy that.

So, the Junkers was shot down, and landed on the other side of the lake. We could just see the wreck from the school, in actual fact. On a Sunday afternoon, very soon afterwards, a rumour went around that we could get to it by crossing the lake and going over the bridge. So lots of us went to see it and we ripped pieces off it. I tore a piece off the swastika, gathered up machine gun bullets, and other things. Some of the boys took oxygen cylinders; you name it, we took it.

Then suddenly, one of the boys said, 'The old man's coming' and Doctor Skinner, our headmaster, was coming towards us – not looking very happy. Lots of us hid behind trees, but most of us were caught.

That is the story behind Peter Blackburn's caning and his introduction to the Second World War. He was young and largely oblivious to the bigger picture of the war but, that said, frequent air-raid sirens were a constant reminder of the uncertain times he was living in. Air-raid sirens resulted in frequent visits to the cellar, sometimes all night, forcing uncomfortable sleeps on wooden slats covered by carpets.

However, not for a moment was he complaining about the broken nights – far from it. From the moment Prime Minister Neville Chamberlain declared, on 3 September 1939, that Britain was at war with Germany, Peter Blackburn – in spite of his only having just entered his teenage years – wanted to know as much as he could about what was happening in the world around him, in his own country and beyond. He wanted to know about the dangers of war, beyond the relatively peaceful and safe corner of the British countryside where he knew he was fortunate to be living. He did whatever he could to gather information, by listening to the radio and reading newspapers in the school reading room.

He recorded snippets in his handwritten diaries, which he was kind enough to share with me for this book. For example, in February 1941, Peter, not even 15 years old, wrote beautifully in pencil, in small, curvy letters declaring the following:

Sun – Sexagesima: The Abyssinian frontier post Kurmuk was captured. Malta was attacked. Greeks captured 300 more prisoners.

Mon – No change in Libya and Eritrea. Italian fighter shot down by Greeks. London had a lot of (100s) of incendiary bombs. 2 JUs [Junkers] shot down on Norfolk coast.

Tues – Moon Last Quarter, 6.07 pm: Italians abandoned Dangila, in Abyssinia, and other posts in Gojjam area. One bomber lost (ours), 22 Italians shot down. A 4,000 ton supply ship sunk used by Italians.

Wed – Enjabara (Ethiopia) captured, and Abyssinian revolt rapidly growing in strength because Dangila was captured. 300 prisoners captured in Albania. Minesweeper HMS *Huntley* reported lost. Strong force of 1000s of Australians disembarked in Singapore to augment the garrison in the colony.

Th – South African troops captured important town of Mega, in Abyssinia, taking 600 prisoners (mostly European) and guns. Mega is an air base. The Greeks reported capture of two villages with 300 prisoners and 50 guns. Large formation of bombers and fighters attacked Berat, in Albania.

Fri – 107 medium tanks captured or destroyed in Battle of Benghazi. Greek press reports that between Feb 10th and 21st Italians have lost 41 planes, without loss to themselves.

Sat – Chief Scout born 1857, Chief Guide born, 1889; S.R. 7.1, S.S. 5.27 – RAF machine-gunned troops. A coastal plane failed to return. Nothing much at Albania because of bad weather.

Now 92 years old, Peter Blackburn lives in Pulham Market in Norfolk, next to the family farm where he was brought up. He has lived there all his life, farming it himself from 1954. He married Alice in 1955. They had two daughters, Joy and Alison. Alison is married and lives nearby with her husband Paul, who has taken over the farm. Sadly, Joy, their first-born had cerebral palsy and died when she was 14. Alice died in 2014.

Peter's childhood at the farm – Street Farm it is called – was far from easy, but he was content as a child and as soon as he was big enough to hold it, his father gave him a single-barrel .410 gun and taught him to shoot – he thinks he was 11 years old at the time. Shooting was what he really loved. 'I had good eyes,' he said. 'It was tough on the rabbits when I was holding the weapon!'

He recalled how hard his parents worked. As well as running the farm, which was their principal role, his father was a special constable. His father managed a herd of around twenty-five cows, selling milk around the village, and cultivating barley, wheat and sugar beet. Scratching a living was a challenge, but their farm was the centre of the community, employing a full-time cowman and other local employees.

When I visited Peter at his home to talk to him, our delightful conversation took place in the comfort of his conservatory, warm and cosy; a far cry from the chill of the home he told me he lived in as a child. He was not unhappy, but life then, he said:

… was a bit of a challenge. We had an old range in the kitchen at the farm and there we had our meals and a bath, every so often. Eventually my father was able to convert a room upstairs and put a bath in there, but even then, we didn't have hot water, there was only cold. The water had to be heated in the copper, which was in the scullery, and carted upstairs in a pail. That was much better. On a Monday morning the washing was done. The two coppers in the scullery were heated up so the water was very hot. The clothes were put into these coppers with blue bags and they were eventually taken out and put through an old mangle and then they were of course hung out to dry, and after that was done, the floor was scrubbed. In those days the floor was brick pamments [tiles].

My mother used to bake bread and in the kitchen, there was a large container on legs which was filled with flour. When she made the bread, it was put in tins and put in front of the range for warmth. The farm was an important place and the young-sters used to love coming there to play.

Peter, without complaining about his three years at Culford, his prep school, was very glad to come home again for good when he was 16. While he was away, he especially missed holding a gun – shooting rabbits and controlling vermin had almost become second nature to him even as a young child – so when he was 17 years old, in 1943, with the Second World War well underway and the outcome still uncertain, he couldn't wait to become involved and without hesitation signed up to become the youngest member of Pulham Market's Home Guard.

The primary role of the Home Guard, originally called the Local Defence Volunteers because its members were all unpaid, was to act as a secondary defence force and to be on hand spe-cifically in the event of invasion by Germany. It was operational from July 1940 to December 1944, with about 1.7 million men and women signed up to it. They were British citizens who were either too young, too old, or too sick to join the services, or who were working in 'reserved occupations' (of which farm-ing was one, so his father was also excluded from conscription to the services).

In addition to receiving training involving first aid, drilling, shooting and preparations for gas attacks, the Home Guard also performed other roles including bomb disposal and manning anti-aircraft and coastal artillery. Over the course of the war, 1,206 of its volunteers were killed on duty or died of their wounds.

The Home Guard held an especially important role in coastal regions – of which Norfolk is one – because, of course, the enemy often made its first approach to land from the sea. Peter was constantly aware, therefore, of Norfolk's vulnerability and the likely possibility of invasion so, while he would never deny thoroughly enjoying his Home Guard role, he did take it seriously.

In his Home Guard diary, early on in his service, he recalled the instructions he and his comrades were given as to what they should do if they were invaded (which shocked and worried him very much, because he wasn't sure he would be able to obey them!) He wrote:

> We were instructed that no prisoners were to be taken, and we should use a bayonet as we were short of ammunition. I had, by this time, shot many rabbits but I couldn't have stuck a bayonet even into a bunny, let alone a human being standing in front of me. I am sure I would have come off second best – can you imagine that, as a 17 year old farm boy?

Of the eighty-seven drills he took part in throughout his two-year service, his first was just three days after his seventeenth birthday on 20 May 1943. He fully appreciated the importance of his role and the function of the Home Guard, but while he was painfully aware of the thousands of people far away suffering in multitudes of ways because of the war – which he cared about very deeply – he couldn't help but be excited and thrilled with his new position.

And why not? He was finally involved in the war, in a position which enabled him to continue working at the farm he loved, learning more about guns and shooting, feeling useful and appreciated, all at the same time. Peter has kept a chronological diary of his Home Guard history which begins on 23 May 1943, when he received a lecture on the 'Lewis Machine Gun'. Of his time, he wrote:

> We always paraded on Sunday mornings. A week after the Lewis lecture, after the Sunday parade, I was given a .303 rifle and did my first rifle shooting at the sandpit in Guildhall Lane. Sand had been taken out over many years so from the top of the pit to the bottom was about 20 to 30 feet. Shooting was done from a driveway about 80 yards away, looking into the base of the pit. This was used frequently for shooting, throwing grenades etc. I enjoyed my Home Guard duties, doing battle drill using camouflage, marching, night manoeuvres, anti-aircraft defence, learning to use maps and how to find enemy positions using radio on the Spigot Motor [a type of hand-grenade launcher], first aid, learning about the possibility of gas attacks, bayonet drills and other aspects of army life.
>
> In those days with the amount of rats and rabbits it was normal to have guns, rifles and shot guns. We did a lot of shooting using the Lewis guns, as well as Stens, .303s and other rifles. I was able to hold my own in shooting, so I was often in the team to shoot against other nearby Home Guard units.

One of the most memorable moments during his Home Guard service came when his unit successfully captured the American air base at nearby Thorpe Abbots – a training exercise, of course, but not a straightforward one and it was good for their morale to have succeeded.

Thorpe Abbots was one of about twenty American airfields in Norfolk in use during the Second World War; all operated by members of the US 8th Army Air Force (USAAF). Between 1942 and 1945 there were around 50,000 USAAF personnel stationed within a 30-mile radius of Norwich, mostly flying and operating B-17 Flying Fortresses or B-24 Liberator aircraft. These were enormous, four-engine heavy bomber aircraft, and Peter recalled on a number of occasions seeing the sky above him simply 'filled' with them. He said:

> You wouldn't believe it today, how many planes there would actually be in the sky at one time. When the Americans went out on their daylight missions there were hundreds of B17s and B24s in the air at the same time. Crashes were frequent, both when they were going out and when the damaged planes returned to base. In March 1945, when the Allied troops were preparing to cross the Rhine, we watched a large number of gliders being towed towards Germany.

However, while Pulham Market was certainly far away from the front line, there were episodes of attacks which he has never forgotten. They could – had they been properly executed – have had devastating consequences. For example, Peter recalled a terrifying day in February 1941 when the Germans dropped nineteen bombs at a First World War air station in the next village of Pulham St Mary. This air station was one of the UK's first main airship stations during the First World War, hosting airships known as 'Pulham Pigs' – so called after a local Norfolk man named it such, after seeing one in the sky and the name stuck. 'Thet luk loike a gret ol' pig', he is supposed to have said.

The air station at Pulham St Mary opened in 1916, and by the time it ceased functioning in 1930 it had employed over

2,500 servicemen and 2,000 civilians. During the Second World War it was used as a weapons dump, housing bombs, and it was also very close to the railway line, which aided transportation of the incendiaries. This made it a likely target and it was attacked on more than one occasion.

However, of the nineteen bombs dropped in early 1941, Peter said that none of them exploded. 'They all missed' he said:

> The enemy bomber was attacked by three RAF Spitfires and shot down. It crashed near the church of another village close by, called Starston.
>
> The pilot I know died and was buried near where the bomber fell, I don't know about the rest of the crew. Some years later his body was exhumed and returned to Germany. The Germans tried to target the air station buildings on other occasions, but as far as I know only one bomb ever hit a building and didn't explode.

Peter drew my attention to his theory about why he thinks the bombs didn't explode when, if they had been 'properly made', they should have done, particularly referring to the enemy's attempt to set fire to the 'Pulham Pig' station. 'We all reckoned the bombs that fell that day were made by the Czechs,' he said. 'The Czechs really hated the Nazis; it is a known fact some of those paid to make bombs for the enemy sometimes deliberately left out the detonator, producing only the shell.' He may well have been right. After all, Czech citizens were some of the most repressed and hardest working in the Jewish concentration and slave-labour camps.

Peter continued, somewhat intermittently, to keep a record of his life throughout the war in the small, red diaries referred to earlier, noting the highlights of his days. By 1943, now aged 17, he had swapped his pencil for a fountain pen but his writing continued to be eloquent, factual and descriptive.

Hardly a single Sunday passed during that year in which he did not attend drilling or a service in church, and on many Sundays he also had dinners in the village hall. There were special times at church when the all services met together to pray for peace.

Peter is undeniably proud of his service in the Home Guard, and grateful that at such a young age he was able to have been a part of the war, albeit at a distance from the front line. However, his interest and loyalty did not end, or even begin to fade, when the duties of the Home Guard ceased to be required at the end of 1944. Far from it. He had developed a quest for knowledge and a deep care for the men of his village who had been conscripted, which was only satisfied in the years after the war through his research, writing and questioning of the men who returned.

After many years of time spent with local wartime veterans, he – together with others in Pulham Market who shared his understanding of the importance of documenting the memories – produced a book called *Memories of Wartime – Taken From Recordings Made by Local People*. It is a collection of sixteen chapters of honest, personal memories of 'ordinary' men who were fortunate enough to return to their village and tell their story. In doing so (as I have written so many times throughout every chapter of this book), they have enabled our remembrance, and I hope deepened our gratitude for the many thousands who simply did not return to do so.

The preface to the book is written by a friend of Peter's called Fred Howard, who wrote:

The content here offers the reader an insight into what it was like in wartime, both at home and in distant lands. We must all be grateful to the people who gave us this rich gift of their memories. They take us into a period of British history that those who lived in those dark days hoped never to have to go through again – but they were revolutionary times that altered the culture of rural England and the destiny of the nation.

The introduction contains words which also articulate the importance of Peter's work in gathering these memories. Written by Martin Ward, it says:

These were hard times for everyone, even those left at home. Life was full of cruel decisions, wretched need and sad farewells that gave the generation that suffered them stature and strength of character that only such hardship, grief and danger can instil.

Most soldiers in World War II were conscripts; they had no wish to kill or to die. But they found themselves facing the violence, misery and suffering that we encounter in these testimonies. Later generations may wonder at their fortitude. The resolve and stoicism we find here shows that most people took each dark day as it came – sustaining themselves sometimes with humour, or with care for others – and sometimes in the way of the Norfolk ploughman – just putting one foot in front of the other.

For anyone who wants to deepen their understanding of what it was to serve in the Second World War, personal testimonies such as those recorded in this book make essential reading. They are not extraordinary, unique accounts boasting of achievement or recognition; they are the honest memories simply of what it was like to be a young man or woman taken from the peacefulness of their world and transported to another with different people, facing danger and possible death on a daily basis. Each story tells of so much more – of the memories Peter Blackburn recorded, six tell of being sent to the Far East, and each of these memories is different, of course, but all are equally evocative.

All those who contributed to Peter's special book have since died so it is with Peter's permission that I have included Wally Newby's chapter about his war, as a prisoner in the Far East, working on railways in China and Singapore. Wally's story is the next remarkable journey in this book.

10

RABBIT'S LOCKER
– WALLY NEWBY

This is a first-hand account of life as a prisoner of war in the Far East, working on railways and an aerodrome. Wally has now died – his story was given to me by Peter Blackburn, who has kindly given me permission to include it.

Wally Newby before he left for the war, when he was about 18.
(Photo kindly given by Mike Newby)

In the words of Peter Blackburn's introduction:

Wally tells a moving story of stoicism, stamina and heroic survival in the face of starvation, exhaustion and disease, conditions of unbearable hardship and unspeakable suffering.

★★★

They were bombing Singapore and bombing us all the way there along the straits, but we were lucky, no bomb hit us. We landed at Singapore and, after a short period, we were captured – prisoners of war.

We were in action all those 15 days. We were bombed day and night and machine gunned during the day with planes – and we hadn't got nothing to put up. All we got was just a few machine guns and few Beauforts, which couldn't stop the Japs from coming. They set fire everywhere and bombed everywhere and all we could do is retreat back – but we lost a lot of lives there.

Some of the fighting was very heavy; and the time we was in there, we had to fall back out. And when we got back out, they started checking who was there and they said that – I lost my mate, I never saw him get killed or what happened to him to this day and no one ever did find him. He must have been buried by somebody out there and he never had a grave or nothing. And that was a big blow to me 'cause he came from the same village as me, his name was Albert Chapman, and we always went together. We were two machine gunners on a machine gun. We were supposed to be one of the two experts on this machine gun, but I was carrying the ammunition to feed him. But I never saw him get killed 'cause we was in the thick of the jungle, as well, and we had to get back fairly quick 'cause we were losing so many people. And they never did find him, they hunted after the war was finished but they found a lot, what was still there, which the Japs hadn't bothered to move about.

One of the hospitals out there – the Indians, they rushed back and took over in the hospital and the Japs rushed in and they killed everybody in the beds and people in the operating theatres. They just shot everybody they saw. Because these people took cover in the hospitals, they just thought, well, we will get rid of everybody and that is what they done. They didn't worry about sick or wounded or nothing, they didn't recognise the Red Cross or nothing. They just went in and killed people on the operating tables as well.

After that was finished, we was rounded up and we marched to a big camp. We was put in this big camp for a while, then after a while we were sorted out there, and we had to go out clearing up the debris and clearing out different places.

I finished up in China, right at the end. I was on the railway for nearly two years and I got posted back. I was ill and had all sorts of complaints and I had to come back to Singapore – which was very lucky 'cause some kept on and some they shipped to Japan. As I come back to Singapore, I tended to get better 'cause things were better there than anywhere. Of course, when we come back, the blokes there said: 'Oh, we have had a hard time, we have had a hard time.'

They had had sort of a hard time, but they hadn't had the hard time we had had. We marched hundreds of miles up in the jungle as well as carrying all the kit and utensils for the cookhouse and we never knew when we were going to get some food. We used to work day and night sometimes to finish the jobs.

There was no sleeping and no rest and no comfort. All the sick used to have to go out as well – if they could go. Course, they used to have to carry some out: you would sit them down and they would break up stones and rocks.

And then we come back to Singapore. We thought we was in heaven because things were organised there: you could get a shower; you could have a wash and the food was for a king compared to what we had. We never had proper food or anything, we had some bits out in the jungle, but at Singapore they got proper rations and they got three meals a day – which we never got the whole time I was on the railway, working. We used to get up in the morning in darkness; we used to go and get our rations and that was half a pint of rice, like porridge. Then we used to have to parade and go out to work. We all had about four or five miles to walk to where we used to work.

We were working the land on the railway lines and we would be making embankments and bringing out the mould on top to bank it up – or we were making cuttings just for the lines to go through – whether that was low or high. Then we had to make bridges over rocks and rivers for the line to go across. We used to have to knock all these trees down into the ground with a big old ram rod thing. We used to pull it up and let it go down from the jungle, we used to cut them up, cart them, carry them in – which took days. And sometimes we used to cut two or three trees down before you could get one that you wanted – and then they kept saying they was no good. And we only had little hand saws so it took ages to cut trees down and they weren't very sharp.

Then we used to work until was time, well until it was time to come home. If they thought we had not done enough, we didn't come home and had to work longer and if they wanted the job finished, we had to work day and night. We had some sort of lamps that lit up – which wasn't very bright. We used to have to cart out trees. The next day they used to blow up the rocks with dynamite. And we had to cart it out, take it up on the railway lines to make hard-standing.

Then we came home in the dark and our huts were just made of leaves; and every time it rained, the leaves used to fall off. And if we got a little sun occasionally they would shrivel up – so we never had a roof. We would lay in bed, such as it was; you could see the stars and it would rain and rain, it would rain for days, it never stopped raining and everywhere is all mud and you were soaked through to the skin nearly all the time. They never stopped for nothing and if you were sick out there – there was no sickness. You might get a day off, but if the Japs see you was about there, they make you get out and do something, work for them in their place, cart water somewhere and fill up a tank for them to wash with.

They used to run us round in a ring to see who was fit. And if they thought you weren't fit and weren't able to work, they used to beat you up. They think that several of you are fit enough to run around, you are fit enough to go to work. But they didn't know how you were feeling when you had malaria: that weren't very good, you was all shaking and felt very ill – and if you got dysentery you was very ill. But they didn't think anything about that, they wanted you to work.

It must be over 18 months that I was there, in the period before I came back. And I came back because I had ulcers and I was a very sick man. I went into camp and I had two operations, there in the camp. One I had anaesthetic with, and one I didn't have nothing at all – and I shouted out numbers; but the time I had shouted out the numbers, they had done the operation, two or three people holding me down. I still got the scars today.

The only times you used to drink was when it rained, you used to catch the rain water and drink it. Although, we used to cut down the bamboo, that used to be full of water and we used to drink that. There was nothing, you ain't got no water, you went out fall down, you never got a drink for the whole day sometimes. You get a mug of tea in the morning and another tea in the night, only just coloured tea water. No sugar, no milk, there was no such thing as that.

Some of the guards we had, we used to hold up a big rock above our heads, for hours on end – and if they saw you drop it, they would come and cut you round the legs, back or wherever they got with a bamboo stick or a rifle, made you pick it up again. Your arms used to ache, you could hardly pick it up, never mind hold it up above your head. Anything heavy they gave you – to lift up above your head and make you stand there until they decided they wanted you back to work.

That was when we started building the aerodrome at Singapore. They had started the aerodrome and we had to finish the railway or the aerodrome off. And they were landing on it and taking off planes.

Well, I can't really remember how far it was, couple of days on a train to get to the place where we went up onto the railway, but I don't really know the distance. We were on these trucks, I mean, they used to be hot during the day, they used to bake you and at night time they were so cold; we used to shiver all night because it was so cold and we was never allowed off the trucks unless they give us permission.

Somebody used to get out and collect the rations and bring it back and dish it out to each hut. Each carriage used to have so many, about 23 in a carriage, an ordinary goods van type thing. There was no seating, I think you just sat how you could. You could hardly sit down as there were so many of you in there. We had four or five days and nights of that, then they dumped us off at camp and then we start marching up to the top of the railway.

One of the jobs what we was doing was that we were reclaiming the land from the sea. We were bringing in all sorts of stuff to the railways to build it up; and then boards were used to bring in big rocks and we used to have to build up this bank so the sea couldn't come in – so they had more room for the landing space for the aircraft. And they used to fill in the swamps: took down all the trees and they claimed a lot of land by filling in all the swamps right up to the sea. They took all the old banks down and levelled it down. They had some bull-dozers which they got doing that, but we used to have to fill all the trucks by hand with shovels and unload them and level it all off. We used to have a break during the day then and we used to leave all at roughly the same time each night and march home, about two to three miles.

I think we still did work seven days a week. I think sometimes we used to get a Sunday off, but most of the time it was seven days and we used to go to Church in the evening – and we used to get home a bit earlier on a Sunday. We used to go to the church service, it was better than sitting in the jail and watching the walls with nothing to do. We would go and sing some hymns which used to make it better for you, you felt better.

Padre Duckman used to lead the service. He was cox for the Cambridge boat race and he was a very short man and the Japs saw he was a little short man and they used to beat him up terrible. He had as many beatings I think as anyone had. I think he was one of the unluckiest men out there 'cause every time he had any clothing and kit somebody used to take him and pinch it away from him and sell it – so he was always without anything. They would steal your stuff, laugh it off, so he was lucky if he had a pair of trousers on. And he did suffer because these Japs they didn't care who they stole off. Some would steal anything to sell it to the Chinese, to get money for smokes or anything like that you could get hold of.

Loads of things was better there, you see, 'cause you could go home and you were in the jail: you were in the dry and you got your meals, which was better, they were cooked better, because everything was in organisation and the officers in charge. They were looking after the food and watching everybody so they didn't take what they shouldn't do because everybody used to help themselves if they could – especially the cooks. They were the fattest men there, they obviously had double rations. They never looked ill or skinny. But there you are, you would do the same if you had the chance. They cooked it, so they used to take what was going first.

We had gardens there and they used to grow all sorts of stuff in the gardens which used to help make stews and soups. They had all this extra stuff, so it was a big bonus to us. We were making tunnels for the Japs to get into to hide up – what they called bunkers, 'cause they wouldn't give theirselves up until they was either killed or dead.

And then, that came out one day, in the afternoon. The Japs rushed us out and they said: 'All me speedo, camp,' and we all had to go back to camp. And they rushed us round, kept shouting 'speedo', which means 'quick', and they lined us up and we marched home and we couldn't make it out. The Japs said they were going to give us a holiday but they wouldn't say to us that the war was over but we thought it must be now – the war has come to an end because there were planes coming over – and they were dropping flares – and they wasn't Japanese planes. In fact, the day after that they said the war was over and when that was over, we didn't believe it. A day later, they did start coming over and dropping supplies of food on the aerodrome for us. We sent parties out to fetch it and we knew that the war was over.

The Japs still kept on guard for another two or three days – because it took so long a time for us to get our troops into Singapore. And, as soon as they got into Singapore, the Japs just disappeared and went into some camps and all the troops then came out and took over. They were the troops that were fighting the Japs up in Burma.

One of the first blokes that came to Singapore was another mate of mine. His name was Charlie Keeble, who ran a fixing place at Harleston (in Norfolk) with his son. He is the first bloke

I saw which I knew out of the Norfolks. We are still mates and when I went to his eightieth birthday party he had a story about me that he told. When he met me out there, he said I was like a walking skeleton. He said he wouldn't have known me if I hadn't shouted out: 'Charlie!' He couldn't believe that we were so thin.

An endorsement of Wally's story was given by Charlie Keeble, and recorded by his son, Keith in 2012:

My father was asked by the military if he would, rather than come home to England, become part of the prisoners-of-war repatriation scheme. He said he would, he knew lots of people from Norfolk, and he would do his utmost to find them. One day, I don't know the date or anything, he stamped into Changi Prison.

Wally Newby was sitting in what he called his 'rabbit's locker'. My father best described him as just skin and bone. He doubted that he weighed more than six stone. Wally said to my father: 'Hello Charlie, you've taken your bloody time getting here, where have you been', and my father said, 'Well we've been a bit hung up in the jungle and I'm now going to get you to the hospital ship which is in the docks in Singapore.' My father told me it was about 12 or 13 miles away. There was no transport, not even a bicycle. The Japanese had ransacked the whole place. There was no fuel, nothing, so my father elected to carry him back to the ship. It took him two days. He got Wally to the ship and they were given strict instructions, no matter how bad the prisoners looked, they were not to feed them because feeding them after the terrible deprivation they had endured for the last three or four years would kill them. He said it was the hardest thing of all, but he did have plenty of water with him and of course Wally was looked after very well along with many other prisoners of war, also from the same part of Norfolk. They all made it home safely and went on to live full lives.

The sad thing about this is that when they spoke about their deprivation and the hard times they had had, nobody would believe them so they went into a period of many, many years of saying nothing, because many of them had been ridiculed that nobody could have suffered like they did and it wasn't until many years later that the whole truth of the matter came out.

11

CIRCLE OF UNCERTAINTY – DR NOBLE FRANKLAND

This is the story of a Lancaster navigator's flights during D-Day and of his post-war journey as a writer and historian, presenting the war as it was for him so that these years are understood, as best they can be, for years to come.

Noble Frankland, pictured in the middle, with his bomber crew. (Photo kindly given by Linda Frankland)

Without a sense of history, people cannot know where they have come from, or where they are, and so have no idea of where they are going.

These are the words of Flight Lieutenant Dr Noble Frankland, as written in the conclusion of his tome *History at War*. A navigator on Lancasters during the Second World War, Frankland saw action during the Normandy landings and over Germany in the latter part of the war, taking part in thirty-four operations.

This chapter tells of the brushes with death he lived through during that time as a member of Bomber Command, one of its contingent of 125,000 volunteers, over 55,000 of whom were killed in service during the war, such were the risks they faced with every flight. The fearful possibility of death with every operation was a reality of those times, for Frankland and all his comrades – terrifying but true, particularly when flying over German cities which were probably the most heavily defended areas of all enemy territory across the world.

Noble Frankland, 11 October 1945 (last day in uniform). (Photo kindly given by Linda Frankland)

Noble Frankland *c.* 1942–43. (Photo kindly given by Linda Frankland)

However, as Frankland pointed out to me, at least in the Lancaster when he was flying he wasn't alone with the fear and uncertainty. He was one of seven in its crew, each man sharing their inescapable apprehension. Frankland felt that it was perhaps worse for the loved ones left behind, alone in their yearning that their sons, lovers, husbands and brothers would safely return.

Frankland was married to Diana shortly before his tour of operations started. He told me she was as strong and supportive as she could be when he had to go off to fly, but he knew the pain the worry gave her. After the war, she said, 'I always knew he'd come home,' but, Frankland pointed out to me, 'she didn't of course, and she hated that.'

This is so important. Each and every one of the members of Bomber Command – and the thousands upon thousands of others serving in all the services alongside Frankland, in countries all around the world – left someone behind. Their nervousness and anxiety were part of the war, with loneliness forced upon them by the extraordinary circumstances of their loved ones having to undertake extraordinary duties outside of their control.

This chapter also tells of what Frankland has done since the war as a qualified military historian, to present as accurate a picture as possible of the war years, in order that something positive should be drawn from it. He felt compelled to undertake this detailed work because, he told me:

> As far as possible generations after the war need, at the very least, to have some idea about the actual madness of war, only that can act as a warning to others to be very wary of entering into it. If I (through my writing and my work) can bring out anything like the truth, I hope it will have been a useful thing to have done.

The word 'useful' here is an understatement. For any one of us who yearn for a deeper understanding of the Second World

War, the reading of personal testimonies is crucial but so too is an appreciation of the military and political situation which drove the decisions that led to the course of actions in all fields of battle during the war. Dr Noble Frankland's writing, therefore, is essential reading for anyone with a quest for knowledge about the Second World War. His respected views are based not only on facts and assessments determined by his brilliant mind but also on experience. He told me that he always wanted to be a historian, albeit as a child his goal was to be a diplomatic historian. He didn't waiver from this and studied history as an undergraduate at Trinity College, Oxford.

It was while studying that he began his training to serve in the Royal Air Force, signing up in July 1941. The air force put him on deferred service, giving him a place in the university air squadron and allowing him to continue his academic work alongside it. Frankland couldn't quite believe his luck. He continued to live in the college three days a week, indulging in and enjoying his studies, while spending the other four days learning about navigation and learning to fly, which, in those days was in a single-engine Tiger Moth, which he described as a 'beautiful little biplane. The instructor would sit in front, trainee in the back, both of us would take to the sky and hope for the best.'

It was during this time that he began to acquire the skills to become a navigator; not something he had ever particularly aspired to, but simply because navigators were much needed and – he said – those in charge:

> [had a] curious idea that navigation was a rather intellectual job, and because I was at Oxford they assumed I must be quite clever, not quite computing that reading history didn't necessarily mean you had the sort of mind required … I had to spend quite a lot of time learning about astro-navigation too, which might have been useful in normal circumstances of aviation, but it is impossible to

line up your instruments with the stars to any degree of accuracy unless you are flying straight and level for a few moments at least, which would simply have been an act of folly whilst flying amongst anti-aircraft fire, that threatened to hit us from below and above, as well as on our port and starboard sides.

And so to the times during Dr Noble Frankland's war, which have stayed with him during the years that have followed, and have so shaped his views and influenced his thinking, for which we – as the recipients of such courage – have a duty to be grateful.

In no particular order, first of all is his recollection of Operation Overlord – now known as D-Day – during which, on 6 June 1944, the greatest landing force ever assembled began to liberate France from the oppressive occupation by Germany to which it had been subjected since the end of June in 1940.

Codenames such as Overlord were established throughout the war years and used in its many different theatres; an essential measure to ensure security for the Allies, and even more so to confuse the enemy. The events leading up to and during D-Day were no exception. Almost certainly, the use of such cryptic language contributed to the success of the operation. For example, for this operation, in addition to Overlord there was Neptune, representing the Normandy landings, during which some 156,000 American, British and Canadian forces landed on five beaches along a 50-mile stretch of the heavily fortified coast of Normandy, in the north of France.

The beaches, too, were surreptitiously named for the purpose of the operation, stretching from west to east. Utah and Omaha beaches were the furthest to the west and these were the ones upon which the US troops landed, Gold was in the middle, used by the British, and to the east were Juno and Sword from where the Canadians and the British, respectively, made their entry into France.

The dispatch of troops onto the five beaches was a staggeringly huge operation. With thousands of men on foot, in tanks, ships and aircraft, it represented the largest amphibious assault ever, an integration of sea, land and air forces, which Winston Churchill called 'triphibious warfare'.

The landings began early in the morning on 6 June 1944. The troops met with heavy gunfire from enemy gun emplacements overlooking the beaches, and the shore was mined and littered with obstacles such as wooden stakes and barbed wire. Strong winds made already challenging conditions even harder. They were worst in the west, where naval vessels were blown off course towards the eastern beaches. The casualty rate was heaviest at the American beach, Omaha. Allied deaths on D-Day alone have been estimated to be over 2,500, with thousands more troops injured.

Dr Frankland's initial D-Day operation began at 2.30 a.m. on 6 June. As navigator, he said:

I had to work like a maniac, with very little time to do anything because our target was to bomb a radar station near St Pierre du Mont, in Calvados, in northern France. Our orders were that our bombs were to hit the target precisely, at a precise time, and we didn't have very long.

Accuracy was paramount if the whole operation was to be a success, and this bombing raid aimed to destroy a German radar station which overlooked the beaches.

However, most of D-Day for me was rather strange. I, and my comrades, all knew – as did most people in the country – that an invasion of France was going to be ordered, but we had no idea when or how. But we should have taken the hint because our squadron's base (I was in 50 Squadron, based in Skellingthorpe in Lincolnshire) was suddenly joined, in early June that year, by a fleet of gliders (flown and crewed by the Red Berets of the British Army). This was really unusual – they were there for a few days, but then during the night on 5th June all the gliders, and troops, disappeared. But, even though this had happened, and even after returning from our first operation I still didn't know what it was about. I think I must have been one of the first to see the liberation of France, and one of the last to realise it had begun to take place!

Every member of Frankland's Lancaster crew had a vital role in every flight. Frankland was one of a crew of seven: a mid- and rear-gunner, flight engineer, bomb aimer, wireless operator, pilot and the navigator. From the moment they became airborne, dedication to duty and unstinting concentration were required.

Frankland's role was to guide the aircraft to its instructed location, hardly going off course for a moment. I could almost feel the pressure as Dr Frankland so colourfully recalled his memories of this unusual night for me – but what made it most unusual was the attitude of his crew. He said:

Usually, we were a disciplined, quiet, conscientious bunch – but on this occasion, the boys were particularly chatty, which I found irritating because, as navigator, I was having to do some quite complex calculations; so I told them off. But they continued to be more excitable than usual, pointing out to me the ships they could see in the Channel, with balloons flying from them. [Large balloons were attached to a number of the ships approaching the beaches, which made enemy attacks more difficult.]

I thought it was a Commando raid – anyway, we kept going and made it to the radar station, duly flew around, dropped our bombs and turned to fly home. Then I heard the boys shouting excitedly again, urging me to look down – then I saw the first soldiers going ashore, and even more ships with balloons. But I still didn't know really what was going on.

After leaving the Channel, Noble recalled the remainder of the journey home was uneventful, and upon landing back at Skellingthorpe, he and his crew attended an obligatory debriefing before falling into bed for much-needed rest.

However, continuing the irregularity of happenings, unusually he was awoken before the allotted time for sleep and instructed to attend another – urgent – briefing. En route from his bed to the briefing room, he happened to hear a radio that was broadcasting words spoken by the King. He said:

I knew then that something important was happening, and it was very frustrating not to be able to stop and listen. But I couldn't of course, and during the briefing that followed we were told that in our next operation we must take extra special care with bombing, so as not to hit our own troops. Then the truth hit home: 'Good God' I thought, after being shown a map, upon which a small area was pointed out to us that we had taken back. Then I knew … we had taken part in D-Day.

The following paragraph contains an excerpt from His Majesty King George VI's speech to the nation, on 6 June 1944. It is printed in full at the end of this chapter:

I hope that throughout the present crisis of the liberation of Europe there may be offered us earnest, continuous and wide-spread prayer. We, who remain in this land, can most effectively enter into the suffering of subjugated Europe by prayer. Whereby we can fortify determination of our sailors, soldiers and airmen who go forth to set the captives free.

This was a defining moment but there was still a huge amount to be done – not least of all, France was only one of eleven countries still in the stranglehold of German occupation. However, the climb back had begun. Furthermore, the Germans had obtained parts of the plan but, Frankland told me, they thought it was a bluff – they thought it was a diversion. The Germans did not believe Overlord could be executed on the scale that the plans relayed so they did not mobilise the defences they needed to prevent the Allied success for which the ground-breaking operation became famous.

'Indeed', said Frankland:

> So much of the day was most unusual. During the previous weeks, we'd been attacking targets in France linked with the operation – bombing bridges, stations and railway bridges – and I thought that when D-Day finally came it would be a 'battle royal'. But actually on D-Day itself I didn't see a single German aircraft: the Luftwaffe simply did not intervene. It was extraordinary – I couldn't understand why. They arrived, of course, but thankfully too late. In the days that followed we flew in defence of the army, who were engaged in fierce battles on the ground, whilst we were caught up in fierce fighting in the air. But the Germans were doomed; the Americans did so much. And after we took Cherbourg on 27th June, there was a constant flow of US soldiers and equipment.

However, returning to D-Day itself, in spite of the lack of enemy presence, Frankland harbours some very painful memories:

> Certainly, I remember some very nasty things, including the falling to the ground of two Halifaxes, each towing a glider. The gliders had army crews on them of around 25 men on each. And all four aircraft went down because of flak. Seeking to avoid the flak both Halifax's turned inwards, crossing each other's cables, and they all went down. I learnt later they were on their way to Pegasus

Bridge, the reclamation of which was crucial because it was an important enemy byway to the landing beaches in Normandy.

Operations over France, however, explained Frankland, were relatively short compared to those over Germany, some of which were for over ten hours. He recalled one particularly long and memorable flight on 24 April 1944, during which their aircraft almost completely ran out of fuel. Their target was Munich.

The route from Lincolnshire was to fly over the Alps to Milan, then, in Frankland's words:

Turn sharp left, and attack Munich, hoping that the German night fighters would be diverted to Milan. Unfortunately, they didn't fall for the ruse. Flying over the Alps was very dramatic because the mountains rise to 16,000ft, which was just above our 'ceiling'. With our full bomb and petrol loads we were flying a very heavy aircraft.

We made it to Munich, though, and flew into the fiercest, brightest maelstrom of anti-aircraft fire I saw throughout the war. I was first alerted to the drama in the sky by our wireless operator: a New Zealander called Bosson who was usually a man of few words, but on this occasion was very excited. As navigator, I had to have blackout curtains drawn, so that the lights I needed to undertake my calculations did not attract night fighters. As we arrived over Munich, Bosson said, 'Come on Bunny boy! (Bunny was my nickname, as it has remained throughout my life). Draw back your curtains, because even if you live to see 100, you'll never see anything like this!' I thought he must have gone off his head because he was normally so quiet. But I did what he suggested, and I did think 'WOW', he was right. Sparks were flying in every direction, the anti-aircraft fire was extremely intense, I could see traces of ammunition shooting at us from all around, including underneath us; all the time having to keep a very close eye on the flashes of colour from the marker bombs; I remember seeing all the colours of the rainbow. But whilst it may have been a brilliant display, it was terrifying. We were exposed and vulnerable to each and every bullet flying around, any of which could have hit our fuel tank, igniting us and turning us into a fire ball …

Wing Commander Leonard Cheshire flying in a Mosquito was the master bomber. He took his aircraft very low – around 250ft. After he called us to, we dropped our bombs, took photographs and turned to return home. But moments after that we picked up a German fighter that 'got on our tail', pursuing us but without firing, even though our rear gunner was firing at him. We had different firing 'ranges' – ours was about 750 yards, theirs was about 1,000, so quite a contrast. This continued for about 40 minutes, during which time we were constantly 'cork-screwing'. (It was our gunner's job to tell us where the attacks were coming from – starboard or port side – so if he said 'Fighter coming in on starboard … stand by … corkscrew starboard go' the pilot would straightaway turn to the right, then to the left, then left again, back to the right twice, and on we would go; the reverse being true if the gunner indicated the fighter was coming at us from the port side.)

During all of this corkscrewing, navigation was simply impossible: my instruments were thrown to the floor and the gyros collapsed. Eventually though, I heard our gunner saying 'He's gone. We've lost him!' It was a huge relief to still be alive. Then I thought 'where the hell are we?'

The procedure at times like that was to draw a 'circle of uncertainty', large enough to include all possible positions. This circle gave me a position error of plus or minus 250 miles. I then plotted the centre and took our position to be the centre of the estimated distance we had travelled in the 40 minutes since I had last been able to plot it. Without telling him how lost we were, I gave the pilot a course to fly home. Assuming my circle of uncertainty was correct, I expected we would soon be flying over the huge Ardennes forest, in south east Belgium that extends into France, Germany and Luxembourg. But it was impossible to know where we were because it was dark, so had to just hope for the best.

I thought I was giving the right instructions to pursue a Normandy course. But by the time we should have been seeing the French coast as dawn started to break, I asked the bomb aimer what he could see and he just said 'Fields'. There was still no sign of the coast or the Channel. Then I saw a field full of parked German Messerschmitt 109s, which might take flight and attack us. Some time later, however, at last, the French coast came into view below us. But as it appeared the flight engineer announced we were practically out of fuel. He tried to calculate 'consumption by boost' and we slowed down … and just, only just, made it over the Channel, finally landing at RAF Tangmere, in West Sussex.

We ground to a halt, literally, as we were taxying in. Our Lancaster had to be towed by a tractor to complete its journey to its parking and refuelling spot. We had been in the air for over ten and half hours.

Just as frightening was an operation on 7 July 1944 when the target was Saint-Leu-d'Esserent in northern France. By then an experienced navigator, Frankland had been given the duty of target finding: calculating the aiming point for the other aircraft, which involved going round the target more than once. After attacking the target and while heading for the French coast, they were attacked by a German night fighter. The words 'set starboard petrol tank on fire' are simply written, indelibly, into his logbook.

This was his Second World War moment of thinking his 'time was up'. Frankland said:

It was very, very frightening. What happened was that suddenly the starboard wing was hit with incendiary fire. That ignited the petrol tank in the farthest engine, and the fire quickly began to advance along the wing. I saw the flames racing along and just thought 'in the next ten seconds we'll all be dead.' But the seconds passed and we weren't! The first thing we saw were the flames; we saw the German fighter later. (German fighters could stalk Lancasters from underneath. Lancasters had no under turret so no downward vision though Canadian-built ones did.)

The normal procedure would be to bail out. But both the pilot and I did not fancy jumping as we had a fear of heights. We suggested that anyone else who wished to do so should bail at once. Nobody did – despite the fact that it was now pretty obvious that our chance of survival was very slim indeed. So we stuck together; we kept going; and ten minutes later we landed, on home ground at Ford in Sussex.

Those were probably the longest ten minutes in my life, it felt like 150 years … during that time the wing began to warp. The second starboard engine quickly burned to a frazzle as well. The pilot dived for about 10,000 feet at one point in the hope of blowing out the flames, but it only increased their intensity and made things worse because we fell very low and couldn't climb back up. So we were completely unbalanced, our speed was falling – it was a very, very marginal situation indeed. As we arrived towards Ford, instructions were being shouted at all of us to 'bail'; but none of us would. Actually, we were flying so low by that point that it wasn't an option anyway, because parachutes have to be at least at 1,000 feet up to open, so any of us who jumped out of the aircraft would have almost certainly died on impact. Instead we told flight control we would have to make an emergency landing. But as we came into land, we saw that the runway was blocked by an aircraft that had crashed, and all we could do was land on the grass next to it. We bumped painfully onto the ground and ran for our lives, expecting the aircraft to explode at any moment.

The other extraordinary feature of this flight was that the German fighter that followed us down in our dive and then flew round us keeping just out of our guns' range didn't make a second attack. Why it should have been so, I did not know then or know now. Guns jammed? Ran out of ammunition? Assumed that we would crash anyway?

Dr Frankland told me they all slept extremely well that evening and the next day visited the wreckage of the aircraft. The huge starboard wing was, he said, 'burnt to a crisp. Thinner than a sheet of tin foil.'

Later that day, Frankland and the crew were flown back to Skellingthorpe, their base close to Lincoln, by a comrade from 50 Squadron. It was the first and only time during the Second World War that he was a passenger. Frankland's war was by no means over, and that evening he was exceptionally glad to be back.

Dr Noble Frankland flew his last operational sortie a few weeks later, on 26 July. By this time, much of northern France had been liberated, but the south of the country had yet to be (it wasn't until the end of August that France was once again its own, with Paris finally liberated on 25th of that month). His instructions were to bomb a railway junction at Givors, a town located in the Rhône-Alpes region of south-east France. The junction needed breaking up, Frankland told me, in order to disrupt German troop movements connected with the Allied invasion of the south of France. It was to be an operation involving about 100 Bomber Command aircraft, of which Frankland's Lancaster was one.

It was, however, to be extremely eventful. Events were dictated to them largely by the weather, which was appalling, making their already challenging and precarious work even harder. While they were waiting to leave Skellingthorpe at 9.45 p.m. a thunderstorm was raging:

It was a terrific storm, with so much thunder and lightning we expected the operation to be cancelled. We sat near our aircraft, waiting, keeping our eyes on the control tower, expecting to see a red 'Verey' light, calling it off. However, nothing happened so we got on board and taxied out to the 'caravan' at the edge of the runway, with the storm still active – huge crashes of thunder and flashes of lightning. When we got to the start of the runway we still expected the red light; but instead we got a green, so we took off. It was a very bumpy flight, the aircraft climbing up through the wind and rain, with sparks flying between the points of my dividers [the sharp pointed instruments navigators used to measure and mark angles and positions on their maps].

Eventually, we got to Givors. It was pouring with rain and still the storm was active. There was no defence: enemy aircraft were evidently grounded. So we ventured to turn on our navigation lights fearing collision more than enemy attack. The master bomber was Leonard Cheshire who marked the target. We followed and bombed and photographed it and began our journey home.

I discovered later that only about four aircraft in that flight had continued to the target. The rest had turned back, which was normally a cardinal sin but on this occasion, they were exonerated and escaped punishment, because conditions were so severe.

But at least I wasn't too frightened of the storm because I thought an aircraft couldn't be struck by lightning, simply because it wasn't in contact with the ground. But some years later I discovered I was wrong – so, goodness, we were lucky! – It was during a chance conversation with a mentor of mine, Sir Henry Tizard, that I found out.

Sir Henry developed the radar chain that contributed to the success of the Battle of Britain. Frankland told me Sir Henry had found out through personal experience that an aircraft could be struck by lightning while in flight. Frankland recalls, 'I was telling him about this particular flight, and he laughed and said, "It is a good job you didn't know!".' Sir Henry had been an experimental pilot in the Royal Flying Corps in the First World War and was thoroughly expert in the vulnerabilities of aircraft in contrasting weather situations.

A couple of years after the war ended, Dr Frankland returned to Givors while on holiday in France with his wife. The wreckage, he said, was still clear to see. 'I found a sign saying "Givors", just lying on its side,' he told me. 'I picked it up and put it in its correct position. I felt then that I had gone "Full Circle".'

As alluded to in the introduction to this chapter about Dr Noble Frankland's Second World War service, I don't think anyone could be better qualified than him to offer opinions about the war and to question and provide important analysis about views expressed by others. His courage in the sky during that fearful time matches the sharpness of his mind, which he has so painstakingly exercised since the war came to a close, in studying the bombing offensive against Germany.

In terms of enabling our understanding of the Second World War, Dr Frankland's contribution through his writing since the war, and also in directing the Imperial War Museum between 1960 to 1982, has been immensely important. He was awarded the Distinguished Flying Cross in 1944 for his services in Bomber Command. In 1951 he received a Doctorate in Philosophy from Trinity College, Oxford, while working in the Air Historical Branch of the Air Ministry. He served as official military historian in the Cabinet office from 1951 to 1958, during which he wrote – with Sir Charles Webster – the four volumes of *The Strategic Air Offensive against Germany 1939–*

1945. He has written many other books, not only about the Second World War, and was awarded a CBE in 1977 and made a Companion of the Bath in 1982. He has been honoured by the French too, receiving the Légion d'honneur for his role in support of the Normandy landings.

Despite those achievements – whatever is written and documented, by anyone – Frankland says:

> People can't really ever understand the war because there are no words that adequately express how one actually feels in the thick of a battle – it is just impossible to convey. I can't even describe how I felt myself.

But what he has told me describes the reality as it was for so many: terrifying happenings that have given us the peace we have today. Of course he is right, we can't understand what it was really like. We can't empathise with fear on such a scale. But that should not prevent us from at least always being grateful. Through the writing and honesty of those such as Dr Noble Frankland we can begin to appreciate the part history plays in where we are today, and where we will be tomorrow.

★★★

His Majesty King George VI, addressing his subjects on D-Day, 6 June 1944, said:

> Four years ago our Nation and Empire stood alone against an overwhelming enemy with our backs to the wall.
>
> Tested as never before in our history, in God's Providence we survived that test. The spirit of the people, resolute, dedicated, burnt like a bright flame lit surely from those unseen fires which nothing can quench.

Once more a supreme test has to be faced. This time the challenge is not to fight to survive, but to fight to win the final victory for the good cause.

Once again what is demanded from us all is something more than courage, more than endurance. We need the revival of spirit, the new unconquerable resolve. After nearly five years of toil and suffering we must renew that crusading impulse on which we entered the war and met its darkest hour.

We and our allies are sure that our fight is against evil and for a world in which goodness and honour may be the foundation of the life of men in every land. That we may be worthily matched with these new summons of destiny I desire solemnly to call my people to prayer and dedication.

We are not unmindful of our own shortcomings, past and present. We shall ask not that God will do our will, but that we may be enabled to do the will of God. And we dare to believe that God has used our Nation and Empire as an instrument for fulfilling His high purpose.

I hope that throughout the present crisis of the liberation of Europe there may be offered us earnest, continuous and widespread prayer. We, who remain in this land, can most effectively enter into the suffering of subjugated Europe by prayer.

Whereby we can fortify determination of our sailors, soldiers and airmen who go forth to set the captives free.

The Queen joins with me in sending you this message. She well understands the anxieties and cares of our womenfolk at this time. And she knows that many of them will find, as she does herself, fresh strength and comfort in such waiting upon God. She feels that many women will be glad in this way to keep vigil with their men as they man the ships, storm the beaches and fill the skies.

At this historic moment surely not one of us is too busy, too young, or too old to play a part in a nationwide, a worldwide vigil of prayer as the great Crusade sets forth.

If from every place of worship, from home and factory, from men and women of all ages and many races and occupations, our intercessions rise, then, please God, both now and in the future not remote, the predictions of an ancient song may be fulfilled: 'The Lord will give strength unto His people, the Lord will give His people the blessing of peace'.

PRISONER OF WAR – FIVE SHORT STORIES BY ALASTAIR PANTON

Introduction

Sergeant Stride was burned to death in his turret. I heard him scream continuously as I was trying to land the burning aircraft. I was unable to speak with him over the intercom. The screams died just as the aircraft crashed, and the turret was a mass of flame when I found myself outside the cockpit, lying on the ground.

These are my grandfather, Alastair Panton's words, taken from a Ministry of Defence questionnaire that he was required to complete after captivity ended. The 'burning aircraft' he refers to was the Bristol Blenheim he was flying, from which he managed to escape before it was engulfed in fire. This happened on 14 July 1940. It marked the beginning of five years in captivity.

Grandfather survived this crash, albeit with horrific injuries including terrible burns to his eyes – he was blinded for over a week. Soon after he fell, he was captured by Germans and taken to a military hospital. According to his records, he was not transferred from the hospital to his first prisoner-of-war camp until December of that year.

Grandfather suffered then, as so many other servicemen suffered that summer and throughout the war; the physical pain of almost being burned alive; the trauma of hearing someone you are close to experience agony beyond imagination; the fear of the unknown when being taken prisoner; and the sadness and frustration of lost freedom.

Sergeant Stride was his wireless operator and air-gunner. His navigator, Sergeant Farrow, managed to escape and was also taken prisoner. I learnt later that grandfather had nightmares following this crash for most of the rest of his life.

★★★

Prisoner-of-war camps sprang up in their thousands during the course of the Second World War throughout Europe, Asia, America, North Africa, Russia and Japan. The experience of POWs would have varied greatly from camp to camp, but one of the most decisive factors as to how a POW was treated was nationality. Russian prisoners, especially, were treated appallingly by the Germans. Thousands died of starvation and diseases such as typhoid and cholera, many were frequently beaten and forced to undertake hard labour, and thousands more were murdered outright – some were buried alive, others were taken to concentration camps and shot.

This was partly because Russia was not a signatory of the Geneva Convention on Prisoners of War, which was written and signed by forty-seven countries in 1929. The Convention contained a list of articles which stipulated how POWs were to be treated and, while there were exceptions, the many countries who had signed up to these rules accepted them. So, while life for most Allied POWs was probably dreary and mundane, for the most part they did not suffer unduly and had access to limited recreational activity and medical care.

Escape activity probably preoccupied the lives and minds of the majority of POWs. Escaping, usually by means of tunnelling, was something they were expected to try to do. It was actually stipulated in the 1929 Convention that while prisoners were required to 'observe military discipline and courtesy', they 'could attempt to escape at their own risk' and, if recaptured, escapees should not be punished, although a short period in solitary confinement ('the Cooler') could be expected.

A few lonely days was a risk most POWs were prepared to take. Official 'escape committees' were established in the camps and the planning and digging of tunnels, while physically exhausting, was often very well organised and sensibly undertaken.

Escaping, however, was not an activity POWs attempted simply for its own sake. Military honour and patriotism were also powerful motivators. Servicemen through and through, many wanted to regain their status on the battlefield and continue to protect their country.

Grandfather was no exception. I am as certain as I can be that early on in his captive years – as soon as his physical strength returned – he would have started to plan his escape. In the Ministry of Defence questionnaire that he was required to complete after his release, he was asked if he had 'made any attempted or partly successful escapes', to which he replied, 'I was engaged in routine escaping activities until May 1944, when I suddenly lost interest.'

What happened in May 1944, I will never know. It makes me sad to think that perhaps grandfather had lost hope or become weak. However, May 1944 was a month before the D-Day landings and even though grandfather – and many other remaining POWs – would not have been able to predict its success (or when it would take place), they may have known it was imminent and this fact would have given him some hope of liberation, so perhaps the need to try and escape through POW-made tunnels would have lessened, if only slightly.

This, however, would only have been the case if he knew of the D-Day plan but, as it had been masterminded for almost a year, it is quite possible that some sort of unofficial intelligence had reached grandfather and his fellow prisoners. Also of huge significance was the fact that, at this time, grandfather was being held at Stalag Luft III where, only two months earlier, fifty of his colleagues had been shot by Germans for trying to escape. This was the mass escape immortalised in the 1963 film *The Great Escape*.

However, for grandfather and his comrades left behind this was not Hollywood. The subsequent execution of his fifty comrades must have been devastating and terrifying. The murders were in clear breach of the 1929 Convention, and I suspect it put the fear of God into the remaining POWs, grandfather included.

★★★

Grandfather was incarcerated in four different camps during his five years of captivity, including two stays at Stalag Luft III. Prior to 1945, it was situated near Sagan in Germany, but it is now in Poland and called Zagan (because of the German/Polish border changes that took place after the end of the war). Stalag III was the camp to which 'serial escapees' were often sent because it was notoriously difficult to tunnel under, largely because the soil was sandy, and the buildings were deliberately raised from the ground.

He was finally repatriated in May 1945, when the war in Europe ended. Although I have no documentary evidence to prove this, I have established through conversations with my grandfather's surviving sons, Andrew and David, that he also completed the 'Long March' home, as described in Fred Hooker's chapter (5), earlier in this book. Only history knows how much time grandfather spent trying to escape, and indeed if he succeeded only to be recaptured. But I would 'bet my bottom dollar' that he spent much of his five years in captivity underground digging in a bid for freedom – freedom for himself, freedom for his friends and freedom so, once again, he could fight for his country.

★★★

This part of *Remarkable Journeys* is not being written to provide an encyclopaedic account of life as a prisoner of war during the Second World War. I am including it to give you an insight into what some aspects of captivity may have been like.

A.D. Panton.

As well as being a proficient pilot, my grandfather loved to write. The short stories that follow this introduction are all written by him. While they are written in the first person (he calls himself 'Adrian Blair'), I cannot vouch for the truth or otherwise in these stories. The truth is that he was a prisoner for five years, there is evidence of his escape activity, and I can hear his voice in these stories. Overall, I think they are a heartening look back to his time in captivity. I hope you will agree with me that they are as enjoyable as they are informative. I am sure this is what my grandfather intended.

Victoria Panton Bacon

I
The Longest Tunnel in England

The first time I saw Grismann was late in 1940. Stiff, cold and extremely grimy, I stumbled out of the door of a '*Quarante Hommes Huit Chevaux*' in which fifty-eight of us, air force prisoners of war, had been travelling for nearly three days from the Luftwaffe interrogation centre near Frankfurt-on-Main (as was Fred Hooker, chapter five).

A wide ring of armed guards surrounded the siding into which our truck, and three others, had been shunted. Inside this ring Luftwaffe NCOs (non-commissioned officers) and interpreters were trying to form us into some sort of military formation; we were to be marched to the POW camp at Bronwitz, which was 2 miles away across the flat Baltic coastland of windswept sand. The Germans were being reasonable and good-tempered; we, enjoying the relative freedom from our cramped trucks, were wandering about talking to friends from other trucks, in no hurry to start.

Before long, the officer in charge of our reception, an Oberleutnant, began to show signs of impatience. The December evening was drawing in and he wanted to have us safely behind wire before dark. It was then I became aware of Unteroffizier Grismann, who had been talking to the Oberleutnant. He saluted, turned from his officer and called out loudly, but calmly, 'Come along, shentleman, please. Form up for roll-call.' He spoke fluently, with not an unpleasant guttural undertone. 'Hot showers and a hot meal awaits you.' A howl of derision arose. 'Hot meal! Showers! My oath! De-lousing and swede soup, more likely.' An Australian POW, bizarre in a pale blue Chasseur overcoat and a balaclava jeered, laughing bitterly.

Grismann's dark-skinned craggy features broke into a grin which closed his eyes. 'No! No! Shentlemen, I promise you. Roast beef, chicken, or some such thing at least.' He turned and strode off, haughtily, down the line.

I was to know the sight of him all too well in the months and years to come. His appearance was military but blurred at the outlines; his strong legs were slightly bowed; he rolled when he walked; his hat was always, a little, on the back of his head; and his trousers, above his scuffed jackboots, bagged slightly at the knees and drooped slightly at the seat. He seldom left us, being continually in our compound; if he had no specific task, he was often there merely wandering round, looking and listening. There was little he did not know, and he was a constant danger to our clandestine activities because his movements were unpredictable. There were many arguments about him, and the differences of opinion were often violent.

Few things upset him, he shrugged off normal rudeness such as those remarks about 'The Third and Last Reich', and his good humour was almost tireless. This was a source of irritation to many, and he was accused, often, of being two faced; he was, as I have said, always with us, usually jovial and friendly; then he would find out something and report it, and another scheme would die. Grismann was doing his duty, and the fact that he did it with good humour made him dangerous. It did not, to my mind, make him two faced.

It was very difficult for prisoners to be objective and it was much in Grismann's favour that he quickly appreciated this, and rarely bore animosity towards those who showed their dislike of him. I came to know him well early on, when I was given two jobs by the escape committee of which I was the member for the block in which I lived. I had to review the organisation in the camp for dealing with parcels from home to see what opportunities there were for smuggling escape material. I had also to 'cultivate' Grismann. The two could be carried out conveniently together since one of Grismann's main tasks was supervision of the parcels store and the distribution to prisoners. We tried to corrupt any German whom, through the nature of his duties, we saw often on his own. The process was a gradual one of small beginnings, small bribes and favours, leading to a point when the German was hopelessly compromised; small returns from the German at first, an egg or a cigar, turned into radio valves and railway passes handed across in terror of exposure. We could not afford scruples.

I soon found out that Grismann was not to be cultivated; he was from the start completely incorruptible and remained so until the end. The parcels store was outside our compound in one of the headquarters administrative buildings, and the first day I worked there I was under Grismann's supervision with another 'parcels officer', Sam Carlton. Sam was a lean, taciturn Canadian with a remarkable ability to see in the dark, as I was to find out later when we escaped together.

We were opening parcels, having the contents checked, and doing them up loosely for handing over to the addressees. We stopped work to make a cup of coffee on the coke stove.

'Have a cup of coffee, Grismann?' I asked casually.

'Thank you, Mr Blair. I do not require it.'

'Oh, come on!'

'Thank you, no!'

'Bit of chocolate, then,' said Sam. 'Or a Players?'

'I do not smoke on duty, Shentlemen, thank you, nor do I require chocolate.' Grismann paused and chuckled. 'Whatever your propaganda says, I am very well fed. Propaganda, poof! But don't mind me. You have your refreshment.'

We said no more. Indeed Grismann left no room for manoeuvre, and in addition we were feeling a little silly at the contrast between the stories at home about German shortages and the reality. Grismann knew all about this contrast and he and the others often used it as a basis for jibes. At that time we were often made to look foolish by our propaganda. In all the time I knew him, he never accepted a single cigarette or square of chocolate or cup of tea from any prisoner. Sometimes, in a prisoner's room which he was visiting for some purpose, he would relax and take off his hat, showing his thinning hair and a line of white flesh above the hat-band, but he always smoked his own cigarette, even if he was down to one of those vile Polish affairs which were sold in the Luftwaffe canteens.

The years passed, and Grismann could now speak a remarkable flow of RAF idiom, though his accent never improved. He was now an Oberfeldwebel; senior to when we first met. Otherwise he was unchanged; he was still cheerful and his trousers still bagged and drooped. Bombing of Germany had now reached serious proportions, but he gave the impression that it was not his affair. The Führer could look after that; his home was too far east for our bombers, and his business was to guard prisoners of war. Except for occasional periods when he was on leave, my connection with him had been continuous for nearly three years, when at Sagan in Silesia, late in 1943, it was broken most ignominiously for me.

Early one morning I was coming up from the midnight shift of a tunnel on which I was working, with Sam Carlton immediately behind me. As I pulled myself out of the hatch, I found myself looking into the face of a triumphant security officer, and a room full of Germans. What had happened, and how they had evaded our well-tried lookout system I could not think. I never did find out, because Sam and I were whisked away to the Cooler, and a few days later removed to another prison camp. I saw nobody who could have told me until after the war, and then I couldn't be bothered to find out.

Together with two other soldiers, Grismann was detailed to escort us to our new camp. The journey passed uneventfully. He made us as comfortable as he could, and took no chances of letting us give him the slip. We arrived at a depressed town, Lublorn in Poland, just after sunset. The camp was on a hill outside the town, and from the railway station the usual lights round the usual wire looked inexpressibly dreary. It was raining slightly. An occasional Pole shuffled past, giving the armed Germans as wide a berth as possible.

'God! What a dump!' Sam muttered, looking up the hill. Grismann heard him.

'Well, Mr Carlton,' he said, smiling, 'you are to blame. We provided a nice little camp for you in Silesia and you would try to escape all the time. It is your own fault if you become uncomfortable.'

'Nice camp!' Tired and irritated, Sam exploded. 'Don't talk such trip, Grismann. What the hell do you think it matters what the camp is like? They are all lousy, and even if they weren't, they are still prisons. We're still cooped up in them.'

There was a long silence while Grismann looked at us both in turn. The two guards looked shocked; while they could not understand English, there was no mistaking the tone the usually mild-mannered Sam had used to their Oberfeldwebel. I wondered for a moment whether Grismann was going to turn nasty, but I should have known better.

'Forgive me, Mr Carlton.' He was now unsmiling. 'That was stupid of me. Believe me, I think I do understand how you feel.'

Sam was immediately contrite. 'I'm sorry I blew up. Thank you for looking after us on this journey as you have done. I'm glad you were in charge of our escort.'

'Don't mention it.' Grismann was suddenly surprisingly gruff. 'I'm sorry that you are leaving us. That is all I meant to say.' He paused and looked at the prison camp on the skyline. 'I am sorry that this has to be. This is not, I think, a good camp at all. It is run by the Wehrmacht.'

He did not speak again, and the bluff, leg-pulling manner I knew so well had gone. At the camp shortly afterwards he went through the formalities of handing us over quickly, without looking at us. He then said, 'Goodbye, Mr Blair. Good-bye, Mr Carlton,' turned and was gone.

With a shock of realisation, I understood; Grismann liked us. Although we had utterly failed to 'cultivate' him, neither Sam nor I had ever been rude to him and we had never made a fool of him. If we had ever outwitted him personally, he accepted this without rancour. Lastly, he was sorry for us, although I think it is true to say that we weren't, at any rate for long, sorry for ourselves. For the rest of the war, the prisoners I was with had never been with Grismann, and I heard no more of him. Towards the end, for two nights, the news mentioned that Grismann's home town was being attacked by Bomber Command just in front of the advancing Red Army, and I wondered if his family were still there. In 1943 it had seemed so safe. After I returned home I met in the Royal Air Force Club another ex-prisoner who had been with Grismann to the end. In casual conversation I was told that his family had all been killed. What had happened to Grismann himself no one knew. Just before the camp had been overrun by the 1st Armoured Division, Grismann had gone off with a small armed party to join a hastily formed Home Guard unit.

In the spring of 1946 I had a long weekend off from the flying training station where I was being converted to jet aircraft. Everything I did was still exciting. The flying frankly thrilled me; and I appreciated the small things, including hot water and well-cut, clean clothes enormously. I was on my way to a dance at Old Sarum, to which I had been asked by a red-haired WAAF officer of the right age. One way and another, as I walked down the long platform at Waterloo to board the Salisbury train, my spirits matched the April sunshine. The sight of a number of German prisoners of war crowded into a train on the other side of the platform hardly penetrated my consciousness or my complacency. I was nearing the end of the prisoners' train when, unexpectedly, I heard my name being called.

'Mr Blair! Mr Blair!'

I spun round, and there, leaning out of a carriage, a grin splitting his face from ear to ear, was Grismann.

'Grismann!' I hurried to his carriage. 'I can't believe it. I am glad to see you.' And I was. 'Are you alright? Is there anything I can give you?' I started to feel in my pockets.

'I do not need anything, thank you Mr Blair.' His attitude to favours and presents had not changed. 'You know how it is. I only want to return home.'

I hesitated, 'Any – news of your family?'

'They are by a miracle safe in the US zone.'

'I am so glad! I heard your home had been bombed, and over-run by the Russians, and I feared for you.'

Whistles blew, flags waved. Grismann's train began to move. I followed it down the platform beside him, but the train began to pull away from me. I asked, inadequately, 'What are you doing with yourself?'

Grismann suddenly adopted a clownish expression of extreme craft and furtiveness. 'Shush! Don't talk so loudly!' The train gathered speed thunderously. 'Don't tell anyone,' he yelled, waving and grinning, 'but I am building the longest tunnel in England.'

II
Meredith

I found myself in many improbable circumstances as a prisoner of war, and wandering round the marshalling yards at Hamburg at night with Sam Carlton looking for a goods truck with 'Switzerland' on it was one of them.

A feeling of unreality had been with us for some days ever since we had escaped by the Rukov tunnel. We were 'out', free for the first time, and the change and excitement after so much dullness was intoxicating. From Rukov we had walked for 60-odd miles to Schweinfurt with only the shortest possible stops, anxious to be as far away from the camp as possible, and from the other escapers, when uproar broke out, as it was bound to when our break was revealed. As we intended, we had taken a train for Berlin from Schweinfurt, the terminus of the German gauge railways. We had travelled to Berlin where we changed our cover stories and identities.

We were now Danish dental mechanics, ostensibly heading for Freiburg near the Swiss border, and we had chosen this role on the grounds that we were unlikely to meet a policeman who could speak Danish or knew anything about dental machinery.

Without any trouble or discomfort we had crossed Berlin and caught a train to Hamburg. Unfortunately, this orderly method of progress had to stop because we had run out of German money for more railway tickets. One of the snags of the big tunnel break was that the escape committee's resources had to be shared among a large number, and our Deutschmarks would only last as far as Hamburg. From there onwards, if we were to reach anywhere near Switzerland, we did so on our own resources. Confident after the ease and smoothness of our journey so far, we were looking for a suitable wagon to stow away in, only faintly aware that we were being highly optimistic. We were beginners;

so much of our attention and energies had been concentrated on digging the tunnel that we hadn't planned our journey in detail. Our general intention was to cross into Switzerland, but how we got there once our money ran out, we had left to chance. Already we had exceeded our expectations. We had imagined so many snags; none had occurred, and now anything seemed possible. Only once, at Schweinfurt two days earlier, had we been completely taken aback.

With our third-class tickets we were seated in the train with about ten minutes to go, alone in our carriage. We were delighted with ourselves at having, as we thought, got clear away from the pursuit and our fellow prisoners. We were quietly reading daily papers for colour, when an urgent whisper, into the open window between us, startled us horribly.

'Why aren't you travelling first class? I am.'

We looked up at the grinning face of Dick Crondall who was travelling as a 'consumptive professor' going to Bavaria for a cure. His face had been burned when he was shot down, and he had managed to make himself look pretty ill behind his dark glasses. Nothing was further from the truth; he was wiry and fit.

'Dick! For God's sake!' Sam gasped.

'It's all right. There's no one anywhere near us. I saw you some minutes ago and have been scouting around. You must have made it here pretty quickly. I'm shagged out, aren't you? I want the train to start so that I can have a sleep.'

'We're very short of money' I said. 'How on earth did you scrounge enough to go first class?'

Dick smirked. 'Well, you know I'm a sick professor. You can't expect me to travel hard, can you?'

'What a racketeer you are!' Sam hissed. 'Just because you are on the committee you swipe all the cash.'

'Racketeer? Me?' Dick looked round. 'Careful, there's someone coming down the train looking for a seat. I'm off! Good luck!' He adopted a melancholic air, and shuffled off on his stick, cough-ing thinly, clutching a travelling rug, his excellent impersonation a ludicrous contrast to his actual toughness.

Sometime later Sam said, 'I wonder where that crook Dick is.'

'Perhaps some kind German has put him into hospital,' I answered, and we chuckled at the thought of Dick trying to talk his way past some solid Nordic ward sister. In fact, none of us ever saw Dick Crondall again. He vanished into the Third Reich, and in the years to come I was often to find myself thinking with a lump in my throat of our last sight of him shuffling consumptively down the Schweinfurt train. It was funny at the time, but then, light-hearted as most of our escape activity was, tragedy was never very far away. We did not really appreciate this – at any rate until the Sagan tunnel massacre. (This is a reference to the 'Great Escape' of 24/25 March; during which seventy-six prisoners escaped, but only 3 made it home. Of those re-captured, fifty were shot.)

Our encounter with Dick had been nearly three days before. Now, in the Hamburg marshalling yard, we continued our search. Scattered around were top-shaded lamps on high posts, and in the dimly reflected light from these we found wagons for Russia, the Netherlands, France and Denmark, but nothing for Switzerland or anywhere near it. We crept stealthily about, but we seemed to have the place to ourselves.

After two hours or so, against all probability but matching the strangeness of the whole journey, we found a tarpaulin-covered truck labelled Freiburg. Through a grill in the side we could see cylindrical bundles wrapped in thick paper which yielded slightly to prodding.

'They're probably bales of cloth.'

'We'd be snug as hell in there.'

'It's an answer to a Kriegie's prayer!'

We whispered excitedly together, our imaginations rumbling steadily, comfortably, towards freedom, not considering how long the truck was likely to wait in the yard, nor how we were to eat and drink on the journey once we had finished our already small supplies.

'Let's look for a way to get in.'

'It won't be easy. We'll have to close the cover from inside so that nothing shows outside.'

Side by side, we had just started to work our way round the truck, testing the ropes holding down the tarpaulin, when air-raid warnings sounded. Uncertain, we slipped underneath our truck and lay peering out into the darkness, chins on the rail, waiting. After a while, anti-aircraft guns erupted very nearby, shredding the silence, and vibrations shook dust from the truck onto us.

'The duty Wellingtons are going over,' whispered Sam. 'I wish they would leave us alone.'

'For once you see eye to eye with a few million Goons,' I replied, and then felt him stiffen, pressing my arm.

'Down! Still!' he breathed. I felt, rather than saw, him lower his head and hide his face under the inside of the rail, and copied him. Measured, slow footsteps became louder, someone crunched within a yard of us, and passed a short distance away. All our senses were in our ears as we heard him turn on the cindery surface, slithering, and plod past us again. This sequence was repeated, and we realised we were lying near the end of someone's beat. I remembered once hearing two RAF sergeants talking; they had been in a marshalling yard in an air raid. I inched my mouth to Sam's ear.

'In an air raid the lights go out and railway police patrol between the lines instead. We'll have to stay put until the all-clear.'

That is what we did, stiffening as our policeman neared, relaxing as his footsteps died away, until eventually the all-clear sounded. On came the lights. Another policeman joined our one, and chattering they disappeared. After a time, as far as we could tell, we were alone. The patrols seemed to have gone, and the only sounds were the clanks of distant shunting. We came out from under the truck, shaking the dust from our heads, cold and stiff in the keen spring night air.

'We'd better get into this wagon while we can,' said Sam softly, but before I could answer we heard a rustle from between two trucks on the next line. We froze against our truck, feeling horribly exposed. A wary head poked slowly out, and a worried, cultured voice whispered, 'I say Meredith, is that you?'

Sam recovered instantly, and said, using the exaggerated drawl of a Canadian aping an Englishman, 'Sorry, old chap. No!' The head whipped back and we heard its body leaving smartly.

'Who the hell was that?' I tittered in relief.

'Some escaped Pongo, I should think, by the sound of his voice. Presumably looking for his lost pal Meredith. How clueless can you get?'

We continued working our way round the truck, looking for an opening, laughing in whispers together, imagining the marshalling yard to be the scene of a large-scale game of cops and robbers, with assorted Allied prisoners of war in the role of the hunted. As we examined the truck, we were constantly looking around, and in doing so I saw two policemen appear at the end of our line of trucks. I pulled Sam round the corner of the truck. The police, who were smoking, did not see us, but one was holding a police dog on a short lead, and the dog, sensing our presence, barked sharply.

Immediately we bolted, running on the far side of the trucks from the policemen and dodging into the next row, most unpleasantly aware of the dog and its fangs. Pandemonium broke out; the dog was barking madly and was answered by other dogs; whistles blew; guttural cries were answered in all quarters and even a shot rang out; a bell began to toll.

We stopped, momentarily, panting, having dodged our immediate pursuers, when, from the end of a nearby truck, the unbelievable furtive head appeared again.

'Meredith, is that you now?' it asked plaintively. It was my turn this time.

'No! Sorry again!' I called over my shoulder as we spurted off. This repetition was so farcical that I found myself wanting to give up. How could one try to be a serious escaper with this sort of nonsense going on? There were shouts and running footsteps all round us by now, and when I tripped over the inevitable signal wire, winding myself, I was grabbed before I could get up.

When I could breathe reasonably, two policemen marched me off. 'Prisoner of War?'

'Yes.'

'Escaping?'

'Yes.'

'Bad luck!' They chuckled, delighted at their capture.

As my excitement and nervous energy wore off, I began to feel very tired. We reached a police station. A cell door was opened to show two beds. Hard as they undoubtedly were, they looked most inviting. I kicked off my shoes and flopped back onto one of them. Tomorrow could look after itself.

As my eyes were closing, I heard Sam's angry voice in the passage. 'I insist on a cell to myself!' I smiled; Sam was giving his familiar, to me, demonstration of not giving a damn for anyone. The cell door opened. He saw me, stopped resisting the two policemen who held him, and was shoved in.

'Hello Adrian!' he grinned. 'Tough luck.'

'What happened to you?'

'Shortly after you fell over I ran into about six Goons at once and was grabbed.' He sat down on his bed and began to undo his laces. 'You know, they told me that the two with the dog who found us were off duty taking a short cut home.' He yawned. 'Oh God I'm tired! I hope they let us sleep for a bit.'

Outside our cell door the sentry's footsteps stopped. There was a faint click as he opened the flap over the Judas hole and he squinted in. We did not look up. After a few moments, he left. Sam flopped back onto his bed, looking up at the ceiling.

'Adrian?'

'Yes?'

'I wonder what happened to those Pongos?'

'Meredith and his pal?'

'Yes.'

'God knows. They will be lucky if they weren't caught. The place was crawling with Goons.'

I went to an investiture at Buckingham Palace towards the end of 1945. The King was working through a large batch of awards that day, and I, with many others, had to wait some time in the fuel-rationed chill of one of the anterooms. Some of the bomb-shattered window panes had not yet been repaired. I met someone who had been at school with me. We chatted. I knew he had gone from Cambridge into the Colonial Service, and I now learned that he had spent the war in the Pacific. I spoke to him about Germany.

After the investiture was over, I saw him again in the courtyard. 'By the way, Adrian, I've just been talking to an army officer who was getting an MC for escaping from Germany. I wonder if you know him?'

'What's his name?'

'Meredith.'

'I don't know him,' I said, 'but I know of him. I nearly met him once.'

III

Boots

This part of my story is not about escaping. It is about not escaping.

Early in 1941 there were some 500 British prisoners of war, the great majority members of the Royal Air Force, in the small camp at Bronwitz on the Baltic coast where I had met Grismann. The winter was bitterly cold, and there was 2ft of snow on the ground. A new bunch of prisoners from the Luftwaffe interrogation centre was arriving that morning, and I was reading in my room, when the door was flung open with a crash.

'Have you heard? Red Marley's here. Now we'll have some proper news.' The speaker, Mackay, a 22-year-old fighter pilot spoke, excitedly. 'What's more, he'll stir up some trouble for the Goons. He won't stand for being pushed around.'

Red Marley had become a household name and legendary character at the same time in a few short weeks in the Battle of Britain, but now he must have come to grief, and been captured. I had heard a good deal about him, and I looked forward to meeting such a famous fighter pilot. I also wanted to see how he would react to the calamitous shift in his circumstances; I was already aware that reputation was a very fallible guide as to how a person would behave in a prison camp.

I soon met Marley. The senior British officer arranged for him to have one of the single rooms in the block I occupied. I was the member on the escaping committee for this block. I knew the senior British officer was briefing him about the general set-up, but what I had to tell him could easily wait until the evening. Early in the afternoon, I was talking to Sam Carlton in his room in another block, when Mackay searched me out.

'I say, Blair, Wing Commander Marley wants to see you.'

'What, now?' I asked. 'I was going to see him this evening.'

'Yes, now. He particularly said "right away".' Mackay was full of importance.

The others in the room were grinning, and Sam said, 'I hear his Master's Voice. You'd better run along like a good dog, Adrian.'

I went back to my block, knocked on Marley's door, and entered. He was plump, medium height and red haired. He looked excited. Newcomers often were, particularly the special ones, while they were still a nine-day wonder; soon they became part of the background, working out their own existence in the drab routine.

'Good afternoon, sir,' I said. 'I'm Blair. You wanted to see me?'

'Certainly I do.' Marley spoke sharply. 'Aren't you the block member on the escaping committee? Why haven't you been to see me sooner? I need to be given the complete gen about the escaping set-up.'

'Well, sir, I thought I'd give you time to settle in. I was coming this evening to tell you what was happening and to find out if you were interested in taking part.'

'Settle in! Interested! What the hell do you mean? Of course I'm interested. As for settling in, you don't think this place is going to hold me, do you? I tell you, as soon as I've worked something out, my name's Walker. I'm off.'

'Oh good!' was my feeble comment to this outburst. I looked out of the window at the heavy snowdrifts, and added, 'But it's damn cold still, and it would be difficult to get very far even if you did get outside the wire.'

'Cold! Rot! Give me ten determined men and I'll storm the Goon boxes, take over the camp. Aggressive spirit. That's what you chaps need. Press on. Carry the war to the enemy. Don't let up. Fight! Fight!' His eyes flashing, he was pacing up and down his small room, three paces each way.

I listened aghast as the series of clichés poured out, all as unpractical as they were militant. I thought he must be acting a part for my benefit. Surely nobody could be thick enough to be genuine in thinking like that. At that moment, as if in ironic applause at this outburst, the sentry in the nearby tower warmed his machine gun by firing into a bank of snow just outside the wire. I had a sudden vision of Marley's ten determined men being riddled by the burst.

'Pooh!' Marley sneered, looking up at the tower. 'That's all eyewash. We'll soon fix that lot. But now tell me what's being planned at the moment.'

I told him about a tunnel we were working on from our block, scheduled to break in about four months, and of three or four individual schemes for one or two people who had been registered with the committee. These individual schemes were in abeyance until the weather was warmer. I ended up saying, 'If you'd like to take part in the tunnel, sir, I may be able to find a place on one of the shifts.'

'Yes, all right.' He was off-hand about our tunnel. 'But I won't be here when it breaks, so I'll take part just to help out. There is one thing. I must have some boots. I've only these at the moment.' He pointed to his flying boots.

'Fortunately, there's no trouble about footwear.' I was relieved to be able to talk about something practical. 'We've just had a consignment of clothing from the Red Cross, and you can have a choice of heavy army ammunition boots or light RAF boots. We have a clothing officer in the block, and I'll tell him to get you fixed up.'

'Fair enough,' he said. 'Tell him to look sharp. I don't want to waste my time. I'll see you again in a few days to register my escape plan with you.'

The next evening, Marley appeared at the door of my room where my three room-mates and I were playing bridge. He held out a pair of heavy army boots. 'Here they are!' he said. 'I shall break them in now. Four miles a day to start with, round the circuit to soften them up.' We listened politely, suspending our bidding, and offered him a cup of coffee, which he refused, saying he was off to get on with drawing his maps.

After he had gone, we went on with our bidding without comment. At the end of the hand someone murmured, 'As he softens his boots, he better toughen himself. He looks as if he's only used to walking to where his MG is parked.'

The circuit was the track round the compound inside the wire, beaten out by prisoners walking round and round. Apart from the cutting wind, walking on it was not very pleasant because the surface of hard-packed snow was like glass. The next morning I saw poor Marley (I regret I already thought of the great man as 'poor') hobbling painfully round in the stiff heavy boots, slipping about. After fifteen minutes he was limping and gave up.

For the next few days he talked much about aggression and the offensive spirit to anyone who would listen. I asked him to come down on a shift in our tunnel with me. We gave him an easy job on the railway line, bringing earth back from the face, but the very cramped space, the stinking air and the dank earth were a severe shock to him. He held us up badly, and was soon shaking with claustrophobia. The tunneller nearer to him suggested tactfully that he'd done enough for the first time, and he was eased out. He never asked, or was asked, to come again. He tried once more to do his 4 miles on the circuit, but the previous day's blisters stopped him after five minutes. He dubbined his boots and said he would wait for the weather to improve.

About five days after his arrival he again sent for me. 'Adrian, I haven't quite worked out the final details of my scheme, but I'll let you know soon.'

'Good, sir. By the way, what sort of a scheme are you thinking of? Maybe I can help. Perhaps I can save you going of over a lot of ground which has already been covered.'

However ingenious an escape plan was, there were only four ways out: over the wire; through the wire; under the wire and through the gate. Whatever Marley had in mind, he would surely need help of some sort.

'No, I don't need any help, thank you. It's all in here.' He tapped his head. 'I've done a lot of chatting to people and heard their ideas.' There was an evasiveness about Marley which made me fairly certain he did not really have anything in mind. As it turned out, he never registered a scheme at all.

Weeks passed and the snow melted. Marley learned to play bridge, and strangely, perhaps for the first time in his life, he started to read a great deal. The boots lay under his bed, dust now thickly coating the dubbin, only being moved when the orderly's broom hit them. Our tunnel was ready to break and, out of politeness, as he was the senior officer in our block, I went to his room to ask him if he wanted to go out by it.

'Would you like to draw for a place, sir? I'm afraid the first thirty places are booked for the workers, but you may care to have one of the next ten places.' The chances of even thirty making it were pretty remote, but people liked to be given a chance.

Marley was lying on his bed reading, holding up his book to catch the sunshine which was streaming in through his window. He looked at me for a moment and said, 'May I think about it and let you know tomorrow?'

The next morning he took me to one side. 'I thought a lot last night about your tunnel. I am very sorry to say I must turn your offer down. My wife is not well at home, and it wouldn't be fair to add to her anxiety.' How she would ever know anything about the tunnel at all, certainly in time to be anxious about it, he did not say. I did not press him.

The metamorphosis from the fire-eating new arrival was now complete. In his Spitfire Marley was fearless, superbly able. Now, after a few months, he was only another prisoner, ready to help when asked, and kind and considerate to all. He read novels continually and indiscriminately, often three a day. As he lay on his bed, there was a constant whisper of turning pages. He hardly knew what he had read. I once heard someone ask him about a novel he had read that morning.

'Red, what's this book like?'

'Oh, it's excellent.'

'What's it about?'

'Oh, it's about a chap, I think.'

The truth is, of course, escaping wasn't for everybody. It was no good, and quite impractical, for everybody to think they should burst their way out a prison camp simply because they had been told it was their duty to do so. It was their duty, but only within reason. To be a successful escaper, certain physical and mental attributes were essential. If you were too fat, too excitable, too clumsy or too nervous, if you were too slow-witted or too slow-footed, then you only stood in the way of better-equipped people if you did try to escape. You were much better occupied reading on your bed like Marley, and helping in the 101 ways in which your aid was required. Lastly, whatever you were, or whoever you were before you were captured was absolutely no guide as to whether you would be a successful escapee. This philosophy became accepted among us fairly quickly, and 'Marley's boots' became a not unkind byword for lost causes and failed endeavours.

In due course, Marley moved from the Baltic coast to the larger prisoner-of-war camp at Sagan in Silesia, and his boots moved with him. Perhaps he clung to them as a talisman. Perhaps, as long as he had them, he could go on dreaming of some daring escape, of getting back home, of bursting into one of the Shepherd's Market pubs calling, 'I'm back,' and listening to cries of delighted wonder from the girls. Whatever the reason, the boots found their accustomed place under Marley's bed.

Early in 1945 the Russian advance into Germany gathered momentum, and the Sagan prisoners were given two hours' warning to leave, only taking with them what they could carry. Marley had agonising priorities to determine about cigarettes, books, food and clothes. The boots were left behind. Well, the war was clearly ending soon, and there was no point in escaping. He could now face the fact that for him there had never been any point in thinking about it. Also, he had his own good shoes sent out in a clothing parcel from home.

In late 1945 a friend of mine, an ex-prisoner of war who knew all about Red Marley's boots, was escorted by the Russians to Sagan in connection with an Imperial War Graves Commission matter. The compound which he and Red Marley had once occupied was strangely unchanged. He walked through the huts, his memories and the atmosphere of the weary years of captivity pressing round him. He passed Red Marley's room and there, lying under the bed, were the boots.

He picked them up and gave them to the first farm labourer he saw, who was delighted to have them. I like to think that the boots, too, were pleased to be needed after so many frustrating years.

IV
Double Cross in Gold

As soon as Grismann had left Sam Carlton and me at Lublorn, which was a prisoner-of-war camp run by the Germany Army, we were marched by a Feldwebel (warrant officer) before the Commandant and given twenty days' solitary confinement for attempting to escape from our last camp. Before we had even sat down in the place, the Feldwebel was taking us to the Cooler.

We were soon seeing a good deal of this man. As one of the security officer's staff, he had a roving commission to thwart escape attempts, and we had clearly been made special charges of his. Relationships develop speedily in such narrow circumstances, and he quickly became known as 'Bavarian Otto'. Very shortly we realised that he would have to be outwitted if we were to escape from the Cooler; but apart from him we were optimistic about our chances.

Otto seemed a likeable enough fellow, which in itself made him dangerous. There was nothing sinister in his round, cheerful face and cropped blond hair, and his large, strong frame looked as if it was only waiting for the end of the war to return to farm work. His uniform looked as if he was always on the point of unbuttoning his jacket. He set the seal on the pattern of our dealings with him when he was leading us to our cells. On the way to the Guardroom, he said to me, 'Mr Blair, I think it bad luck to keep on getting caught escaping, but the odds are against you.' I was flattered that he had learned my name so quickly. 'You understand, I know,' he smiled, 'That my job is to keep you here, and I shall do my best.'

When we arrived at the Guardroom, he threw open the door, and announced us to the guard commander like a toast master at a banquet. 'Two British airmen, Herr Oberfeldwebel!' he cried. 'You are honoured. You may not think it to look at them now, but they have a most dangerous reputation.'

We did, indeed, look unimpressive; we had not had a chance to shave for two days; my tunic had been burned a bit when my Spitfire was shot down three years before, and was now in shreds; and the only sign that Sam was in the RCAF was the 'Canada' flash sewn clumsily onto the shoulders of his Polish tunic.

'They are not to be trusted in any way,' he went on, and added, turning and grinning at us, 'and that, they will take as a compliment.'

From the Guardroom a communicating door led into a narrow passage off which eight cells opened. Otto threw open this door with a flourish, laughing, 'Your rooms, gentlemen. Choose as you wish.'

Each door had a narrow open transom across the top. We chose the two cells on opposite sides of the passage at the end. They were farthest from the Guardroom, and we could talk without difficulty across the passage. 'We'll take the end ones,' I said, playing his game. 'They will do nicely, thank you very much.'

'Suit yourselves,' Otto returned. 'Views of the sea are guaranteed with all our rooms. Make yourselves at home. Our service is always at your disposal, and I myself will be around constantly.' Chuckling, he strode away as our cell doors were locked and bolted.

Sam was soon at his transom. 'Adrian?'

'Yes?' I came to my transom in my turn.

'Watch that joker. He's friendly enough, but it's friendship with a purpose.'

Soon it was all too clear that, while we could rely on the general routine of the organisation, the movements of Otto himself were unpredictable. He would come to our cells and chat about all sorts of things; communism, colonies, his home and ours, and with Sam a Canadian he would play the minority people's tactic, suggesting that he, a Bavarian, was dragged into the war at the heels of the Prussians just as Canada had been involved by the British. At our meal times he sometimes appeared with a piece of sausage or cheese to supplement our scanty and dreadfully dull food. He would appear at exercise times and pass the time of day with us.

We met these advances politely, but were careful to give nothing away. The whole time he was with us, we were aware that Otto's eyes and ears were constantly on the alert for clues. As this is a story about our relationship, mine in particular, with Otto, I only need to sketch the outline of our escape plans.

At night, our passage door into the Guardroom was left open, presumably so that the guards could hear if we were up to anything. We planned to crawl from this door to the front door of the Guardroom under the cover of the furniture. Sam was an expert lock-picker, and could unlock the cell doors. What he could not do was draw the bolts on his own door, and this was my job. My idea was to take one side of my metal bed-frame, fix a loop of string to the end of it, poke the metal beam through my transom, catch the loop over Sam's bolt-heads, and pull them open.

During the last of the guards' day shifts, when the passage door was still closed, we could reasonably expect to be left alone. One evening I went to try out this idea. I had just succeeded in opening and closing Sam's bolts, and was about to bring the beam back through my transom in triumph, when the passage door was unlocked quietly, and Bavarian Otto was there. I was caught.

Otto's jaw dropped, he flushed suddenly, and for a moment a look of sharp anger crossed his features. Then he pulled himself together as he closed the door, forcing himself to smile. 'So, Mr Blair!' he said. 'What have we here?'

I slipped the loop of Sam's bolt, and withdrew into my cell with the beam. Otto unbolted and unlocked my cell door and came in. I sat on a stool, rubbing my right wrist which was aching from the weight of the beam, feeling a bit silly as I always did when a German caught me out. Otto looked down at me, smirking. 'I came at the wrong time I think. Please tell me, what are you trying to do?'

I resisted the desire to make some facetious crack, and said, 'I was seeing if I could open the bolt of the cell opposite.'

'And did you manage to do so?'

'No,' I lied.

'But I do not understand. If you had opened the bolt, what then? How do you think to unlock the cell door? And the door into the Guardroom?'

'I have no idea,' I lied again. 'I just hoped …'. I paused, hoping for a plausible answer.

'Yes, Mr Blair?' Otto prompted me, and inspiration came. It suddenly occurred to me that Otto had only visited us by day so far and did not know about the passage door being left open at night.

'Well, it does sound unlikely, but, if the guards forgot to lock the cell doors and the passage door, all I would have to do would be to draw the bolts of the cell door for us to reach the Guardroom.'

'I see,' Otto was smiling now, relieved that we appeared to have no immediate plans to escape. 'And what about Mr Carlton? How is he helping you?'

'He is not taking part in all this yet,' I lied again. 'Twenty-one days is enough for him. And for that matter, it is for me,' I added, looking straight at him. 'Do you have to report this?'

Craftiness spread over Otto's chubby face. 'It is, of course, my duty to do so, but perhaps this time, as little appears to have been done, I could forget it. The Commandant, I know, would be severe with you. Yes, perhaps …', he paused, and his eyes moved to the table beside me where a small gold crucifix on a thin neck chain was lying. My mother had given it to me. I wore it almost all the time, but I had taken it off to avoid catching it on the transom while I was working on Sam's door.

'That is a lovely thing,' Otto said softly. My girlfriend very much likes things like that, and they are not easy to buy, you understand.'

I was being asked to buy Otto's silence with my crucifix, and I felt a shaft of dismay. My crucifix was being balanced against another stretch of solitary and probably our hopes of getting out of the place. I picked up the crucifix and chain, and, feeling very disloyal to my mother, passed it to Otto with as good grace as I could muster, saying, 'Do have it. I hope your girlfriend likes it.'

After a few more words, Otto went out, leaving me feeling pretty mean. In a few minutes I had told a series of thumping lies and had been disloyal. I was used to the lying by now, but I did mind the disloyalty.

As soon as Otto had locked the passage door behind him, Sam was at his transom. 'Say Adrian, what's going on?'

I told him, cursing about losing my crucifix.

'That's too bad, but I guess you had to do it.'

'Do you think Otto will keep quiet?' I asked.

'I don't know. I don't trust him not to do his duty, any more than he trusts us, which is as far as I can throw him, and he must weigh about a hundred and ninety pounds.'

I thought for a moment. 'Sam, he may well be trying to lull us into a false sense of safety. For the first time I noticed the geniality didn't reach his eyes. In case Otto is going to queer our pitch let's go as soon as we can before he can lay anything on us.'

'Too true. We'd better go this evening.'

Night came. As soon as the first night guard had visited us and left the passage door open, we slipped out of our cells with ridiculous ease. In the Guardroom two of the off-duty guards chatted idly by a stove. From the passage door, our boots round our necks, we crawled gingerly round the walls of the Guardroom, hidden from the occupants by a row of lockers and a key cupboard.

The main door into the Guardroom opened onto a long counter, and Sam was just reaching the end of it when the door was flung open, towards us. We froze where we lay, hidden but able to see nothing. Several people crowded in through the door. From the clicking of heels and the scrambling about, one of them was obviously an officer. This the guard commander confirmed by saying, 'Good evening, Herr Hauptmann.'

'Good evening, Oberfeldwebel.' The officer sounded in good spirits. 'You may be interested to know that your two prisoners are up to their tricks. My Feldwebel here caught one of them this evening with a piece of his bed trying to open the bolts of the cell opposite his.' Herr Hauptmann was obviously the security officer, and we heard Bavarian Otto chuckle complacently. So he had double-crossed me out of my crucifix! 'Come with us to the cells, Oberfeldwebel' the security officer went on, 'We shall take away their beds. They must sleep on the floor, and tomorrow the Commandant will deal with them.'

At this point Otto must have looked at the door to the cell passage. We heard him say urgently, 'Herr Hauptmann! The door to the passage – it's open!'

'Oberfeldwebel!' The officer's voice had a sharp edge. 'Why is that door open?'

The Oberfeldwebel, who was only doing his job in his turn on the roster, was obviously out of his depth in all of this. 'The door?' he asked, puzzled. 'But it is always, by order, open at night.'

We heard a muttered oath and rapid footsteps. Sam peered round the end of the counter and saw the security officer, Otto and party disappearing round the other end. He crawled quickly to the door, which was ajar, eeled round it, and was gone. I followed.

Outside the Guardroom we hared across the 30 yards of our daily exercise area to the outside wall which was only 8ft high, scrambled over it under the two strands of the barbed wire on top, slipped across a road and into a large spinney. We paused to put on our boots and I felt my muddied socks squelch as I did so. As Sam, with his wonderful night vision, led a way through the trees, I heard the rumpus of discovery break out. A cool breeze played on our hot, excited faces.

By a series of outrageous flukes we had outwitted Otto. I bore him no animosity for his double-cross in itself; I had lied to him blithely and would have cheated him in any way that I could. But he should not have pretended to seal the bargain with my crucifix. I cursed him for the unnecessarily dirty trick in taking it off me for nothing. I cursed him soundly, but in a curiously objective manner.

I was soon recaptured, and my belongings from my cell at Lublorn were eventually returned to me. Among them, in a small box, was my crucifix and chain. I have always wanted to thank Otto, and apologise for doubting his sense of fairness, but I never saw him again.

V
Jealousy is a Short Straw

When Sam Carlton and I broke out of the Cooler at Lublorn, we walked hard across country for about five hours before dawn, and six afterwards. We were making for Danzig or Gdynia, hoping to stow away in a Swedish ship. By midday, when we were possibly 25 miles from Lublorn, we were very tired, and soaked by steady frontal rain. We came upon a large Dutch barn, three-quarters full of hay, some 200 yards from a farm house.

We slipped unseen into the barn, clambered up into the middle of the hay, and thankfully made individual nests in the straw. It felt wonderfully soft and warm. I was falling asleep as I lay down, and the last thing I remember was thinking it would have been better if we weren't so close to the farmhouse.

A dog barking at the bottom of the pile of hay woke me at dusk. I peered out. In the farmhouse, lights were on and a battered looking Opel saloon stood outside the front door. It looked as if the farmer and his dog had been out for the day and had returned. Sam's lean face appeared beside mine. 'I would like to throttle that damned dog,' he muttered. 'I wonder if they have had any alarm about escaped prisoners.'

I wanted more sleep, it was still raining, and the hay was warm. Lazily I said, 'We'll soon find out. Let's wait and see. We may have to do a sudden bolt.'

We did not have to wait long. The door of the cottage opened and three men appeared, one with a gun and two with pitchforks. The German farmer had called out his labourers. He came to the side of the barn where his dog was barking, peering up. It was now nearly dark. He cocked his shotgun.

'Who is there?' The dog's barking reached a crescendo. 'I know someone is there, escaped prisoners of war.' The farmer's voice was shrill with excitement. His two labourers were out of sight, probably on the other side of the barn. 'Speak up. Who are you?' He fired his gun, pellets tinkled off the roof of the barn, and I nearly jumped out of my skin. 'I advise you to give yourselves up before the police arrive. It will be better for you.' I suspected he wanted the glory of capture. Thinking hard, I tried to find a way out of the trap.

'We'd better do something before the police arrive,' Sam whispered into my ear. 'Let's make a jump and bolt for it.'

'I don't fancy jumping down from here,' I whispered back. 'It must be 18ft high at least, and that chap is ready to plug us full of pellets. If one of us gives himself up, pretending he's alone, the other might be able to sneak off.'

The farmer was shouting 'Surrender! Surrender!' The dog sounded as though it was going to tear its throat open.

'I don't like splitting up.' Sam's face was a pale blur. 'But I think perhaps you are right. Let's pull straws.' He fumbled at his side and then held out his hand, two straws pinched between thumb and forefinger. I drew mine and we compared lengths. Mine was half the length of his.

'All right,' I whispered. 'Good luck!' I crawled to the edge of the haystack and shouted, 'I surrender! Don't shoot! Call off your dog and I will come down.'

'Where is the other one?' The farmer was nearly choking with excitement. 'Where is your comrade?'

'I do not know,' I replied. 'I hurt my ankle and hid here. He went off and left me.' I introduced a note of bitterness, and heard Sam mutter, 'Brilliant stuff' beside me. 'Please light up the side of the stack and I shall climb down.'

The two labourers had joined the farmer, and I leaned out over the edge of the hay into the light of their torches, edgily conscious of the farmer's trembling trigger-finger. 'Take care!' the farmer yelled. 'I shall shoot if you try any tricks.'

'Please put down your gun,' I replied, felt Sam's farewell squeeze on my calf, and climbed down, acting a painful ankle. 'I know I am beaten. Hold that dog back.'

When I reached the ground, the farmer and one of his labourers grabbed me, and the other held the dog. I leaned heavily on my captors, groaning as we moved in a clumsy body to the farmhouse. In the big kitchen the three men and the farmer's wife stared at me, hardly taking their eyes off me for half an hour until the police arrived. The dog remained silent and I was fairly sure

Sam had made his getaway. As the police led me handcuffed out of the house to the car, I wondered if he was near enough to watch. Probably not.

Back at Lublorn I had a reception which puzzled me and bothered me. I had committed what I considered to be a routine irritation, but the Commandant's towering rage and evident uneasiness when he saw me seemed out of character and context. He was a lean, handsome old man, whose monocle suited him, and, when I had seen him before, he had been almost gentle. Now I was clearly doing his health no good at all.

I spent five days in my cell without anything happening. A guard stood in the open doorway of my cell, day and night, refusing to talk to me and obviously scared by the threatening vehemence of his instructions. Then, during the sixth night, I was woken from a restless sleep by the Oberfeldwebel guard commander and a soldier who took my clothes away, leaving me only the very tattered striped undershorts in which I had been sleeping.

There was something very odd going on; it was reasonable for some excitement to have broken out when I was first brought back, but the atmosphere which bordered on hysteria had been difficult to understand; then had followed the strange lull of five days; now the sudden removal of my clothes in the small hours. The more I thought about it, the less I liked the look of things. I smelt trouble, and the uneasiness made me cold.

Daylight came. I asked the passing guard commander for breakfast. I was instantly told it was forbidden, so instantly that depriving me of breakfast must have been part of some arrangement already made. I still had no clue as to why all this was happening, but I soon learned. A guard commander, who had behaved in a relatively friendly manner to me, had come on duty and – looking at me uneasily – handcuffed my hands behind me.

'Oberfeldwebel, what is happening?' I asked. He went into the passage and looked round.

'You are going to be interrogated,' he whispered, 'by special security officers. The Commandant thinks that you and your friend are agents connected with the Polish underground. I beg of you not to say I told you.'

'Thank you!' I whispered back, summoning a grin. 'I'll put in a good word for you when we have won the war.' Agents! So that was what all the flap was about. I could be in deep trouble.

Shortly after this, some sinister-looking people in plain clothes arrived, accompanied by some brown-uniformed Field Police and the Commandant. They quickly reconstructed our method of opening the cell doors, using Sam's homemade skeleton key. I was most impressed with their speed and impassive competence, which did not lessen my uneasiness. Not a word was said to me until they had finished, when a Field Police major turned to me and asked, 'Was that how you opened the cell doors?'

'Yes. You are exactly right,' I replied. I didn't want to antagonise these gentry, and 'Gestapo' was a word I didn't want to even think about at that moment.

'Thank you for your answer.' The major nodded pleasantly to me, said something to his colleagues about, 'No help from anyone else, you see', brushed past the Commandant without a look, and left, followed by the rest of the party. Here was an extra puzzle; why the reasonable attitude to me, and why the ignoring of the Commandant?

Within minutes a field policeman came back. 'Right, Lieutenant Blair, come please.' He took my arm and led me, handcuffed, nearly naked and barefooted as I was, down the passage past many curious eyes. He ushered me through a door into a blaze of light. Blinking, I saw a small dais, and was told to stand on it. I was facing a horseshoe of arc lamps, and questions started coming at me from figures who were only vague outlines in the gloom behind the glare. I felt sick with apprehension; what would I have to go through before I convinced them that I knew nothing about the Polish underground?

It was very hot under the lights.

This was by no means my first interrogation, even if I had never seen such elaborate arrangements. My policy was to be polite and to refer to the military code of conduct. This usually worked because I never knew anything worth much. This particular inter-rogation lasted a long time, and went round and round, with the same questions.

'You are Flight Lieutenant Blair?'

'Yes.'

'Aged 25?'

'Yes.'

'Why do you escape?'

'It is my duty. I am sure you understand that, gentlemen.'

'What is the British organisation for helping prisoners of war?'

'Gentlemen, I do not wish to appear discourteous.' It was impor-tant to keep any hint of sarcasm out of this line. 'But I am under orders as a British officer to reveal only my number, rank and name.'

'Thank you. We, of course, understand, but perhaps you will answer some simple questions?' And then, as I inevitably relaxed, 'What is your connection with the Polish resistance?'

This question, and others like it, kept popping up at odd times against a background of innocuous subjects. I made one error of judgement when I was asked if I found it difficult to fill in my time as a prisoner. I replied, 'Not at the moment', smiling, but no one laughed. I felt flustered, off my balance for a time, and the ques-tions sped up from all around the horseshoe.

Apart from this mistake, I answered politely, or politely declined to answer. Slowly a feeling of success began to grow in me after being so worried at the start. The interrogation had been reason-ably easy to manage because I was, in fact, innocent of anything except trying to escape.

I heard a door behind the interrogators open and someone walked to the back of the lights. The questions stopped, and I vaguely saw the row of interrogators lean towards each other in turn, as if they were passing a message round. The spell was broken. I relaxed, sensing that the interrogators had had enough, when my complacency was rudely shattered. A girl's voice, clear and full of contempt, came out of the shadows.

'You've no idea how stupid you look.'

I jumped, feeling horribly exposed in my tattered under-shorts under the lights, my hands still handcuffed behind me. I hung my head in embarrassment, wondering how many other women were there. There was some unkind laughter, but to my great relief I was soon led back to my cell. The interrogators had been having some fun at my expense to finish on a high note.

Back in my cell, my clothes were waiting for me, and the handcuffs were removed. I was terribly thirsty. As I was finishing some food, the Field Police major appeared in the doorway.

'I have finished my investigation.' He smiled faintly. 'It was reported to me that a couple of dangerous agents were at work here. I had already decided that the report was ridiculous when …'. He paused here and looked sharply at me, ' … we received a message to say that your friend Flight Lieutenant Carlton arrived at the British Embassy in Stockholm yesterday.'

When he said this I felt my face burn and my stomach writhe as I experienced a most sharp and ignoble pang of jealousy. I hope I never have such a feeling again. The outline of the major's face became blurred, and, as if from a distance, I heard him saying, 'When we heard this, we knew, of course, that you were in truth only trying to escape, and had no subversive intentions.' He turned away, smiling thinly. He was well aware of my anguish.

We had drawn straws. Sam had left that barn and arrived in Stockholm. He was free and I was in this lousy prison camp. Later, when the sharpness of my envy began to die down, I realised that the major had from the start thought the Commandant was a fool, and soon guessed that I was only what I professed to be – a bona fide prisoner of war.

Later, too, something else besides jealousy began to rankle. I began to brood about the various retorts I could have made to that girl, instead of gaping foolishly.

I have been brooding about that, on and off, ever since.

EPILOGUE

'I am so proud of him,' said Ray. 'It's really important we remember what my brother and his friends went through, for the rest of us. If we write up their real stories, surely the war will be remembered for at least a bit longer, won't it?'

How could I disagree? In writing this book, I have embarked on a 'remarkable journey' all of my own. It is a journey of discovery I am compelled to share because they are not my stories; they belong to others who want their memories to be shared, so minds are opened and memories are not lost. Ray worried about his elder brother, Ronnie, every day of the war while he was away, and both lived with the consequences of war for the rest of their lives.

A chance encounter inspired this epilogue. If I had any doubts at all that the remarkable stories I was so privileged to be hearing should be properly documented, they were dispelled after I met Raymond Edwards.

This memorable, delightful and significant meeting took place at Beccles Bookshop in Suffolk, in early 2018. I had been invited there for a book signing of my grandfather's Second World War memoir, *Six Weeks of Blenheim Summer*, which was published in 2014.

Ray entered the shop, telling me he had seen the poster saying I was there that morning, and came in because he, too, had a Second World War story. He was a 'war child' himself, but he didn't want to tell me very much about his own memories (as fascinating as I later discovered they were); instead, he wanted to talk to me about his elder brother, Ronnie.

I later met Ray at his home. There I had time to listen to his reflections and learn more about Ronnie. 'Ronnie took part in thirty operations, as a rear-gunner on Lancasters. The most frightening operation,' Ray told me, was during D-Day near Caen, during which two out of four of the aircraft's engines were blown out, and eighty holes were made in the fuselage – each one large enough to put a 'fist through'. All the while, Ronnie was seated in the lonely Perspex 'bubble' that was meant to offer protection. He was repeatedly shot at, resulting in a piece of shrapnel getting into his turret, which circled around him within it.

On this occasion, an emergency landing saved the lives of all seven crew, and 'how fortunate they were,' said Ray:

> The Lanc was so badly damaged it never flew again. Ronnie knew, beyond doubt, then, how lucky they were with their pilot. He always told me how thankful he was to him.
>
> He was an immensely skilful and brave pilot. Ronnie told me he used to fly the aircraft as if it were a 'boat in the sea', always tipping the plane, ensuring it wasn't level for a moment. This would have been very dangerous in itself but probably saved their lives – they tipped a lot, so Ronnie could see what was going on underneath the aircraft too – the only way to do this was by 'tipping' and 'yawing', and 'corkscrewing'.

When Ronnie died in 1994, he was 70 years old. Ray told me he had long suffered with back ache and pain due, in part, he always thought, to the very cold conditions he had had to cope with during his operations, some of which – usually those over Germany – lasted for up to ten hours. 'It was tough for dear Ronnie', said Ray:

> Rear-gunners must be remembered … they were the prime targets in these huge aircraft, they were the crew member usually to be shot at first. It was tough, too, because they were the only ones who could not get up and move around; not only did they get stiff and cold but they couldn't use the aircraft Elson either – resorting to filling up old beer bottles, hurling the 'full' ones out of the plane, with a bit of excitement wondering if they would land on the head of a German!

As with so many Second World War veterans, Ray told me that it wasn't for many years after the war had ended that Ronnie began to talk about what he had been through. And, in spite of his pain, he did not complain. Far from it, Ray said, instead he spoke in praise of his pilot – and of the opportunity it gave him to sometimes 'see the sunset twice', because often they would leave just before sunset and 'fly into the cloud above the setting sun' and when they gained their altitude, they saw the sun set again.

'Ronnie was my big brave brother from the moment the war started,' said Ray:

> I remember once a flight of German bombers went overhead near where we lived (in our tiny Suffolk village of Uggeshall), dropping hundreds of incendiaries over the brussels sprouts in the fields. The little bombs started exploding, but it didn't

stop Ronnie going into the field to stamp on them. When he went home later in badly burned clothes our mother was really upset.

So determined was he to be in the RAF he tried to sign up six months before his eighteenth birthday – he was too young – but went off as soon as he could after reaching the right age …

And Ray's war? He was 6 years old when war was declared and 12 when it ended. These formative years have stayed with him forever. Even as a child, in deepest Suffolk, war could not be escaped:

I remember, when we were at school one day, a huge flight of American fighters circled overhead – lots of B-24s, Liberators. It was very noisy and then there was an awful crashing, crunching sound – two had collided and fallen to the ground. It happened not far from our school, we could see and smell the smoke. Not long after the bombs they were carrying exploded too … there was debris all over the place. I've still got a little bit of shell from one of the planes (awful isn't it, but that's what children did during the war, we all did it …)

Thirty-seven people died that day – all the crews and others who got burnt trying to rescue them. What a terrible memory.

Ray also told me about the 'Secret Home Guard', which he discovered after the war was operating almost on the doorstep of their family home:

Unbeknown even to his wife, a chap who worked on our farm was a member of this secret unit; a sort of guerrilla unit of trained killers, commissioned by Churchill, who operated in areas of risk – of which his part of Suffolk was considered to be because of its proximity to the coast.

After the war, I discovered the underground Nissen hut in which this man based himself during his covert times on duty.

The Nissen hut is still there, Ray told me. 'World War II will always be with us,' he said. So we must 'remember them'.

BIBLIOGRAPHY

Published Books

Bennett, Air Vice Marshal D.C.T., CB, CBE, DSO, *Pathfinder – Wartime Memoirs* (Frederick Muller, 1958).

Bramson, Alan, *Master Airman – A Biography of Air Vice Marshal Donald Bennett* (Airlife, 1985).

Crabb, Brian James, *The Forgotten Tragedy – The Story of the Sinking of HMT* Lancastria (Shaun Tyas, 2002).

Frankland, Noble, *History at War – The Campaigns of an Historian* (Giles de la Mare, 1988).

Gunston, Bill, *Aircraft of World War 2* (Octopus, 1980).

Jackson, Archie, *Pathfinder Bennett – Airman Extraordinary* (Terence Dalton, 1991).

Mann, Michael, *Regimental History of 1st the Queen's Dragoon Guards* (Michael Russell, 1993).

Panton, Alastair, *Six Weeks of Blenheim Summer* (Biteback, 2014).

Randall, John, & M.J. Trow, *The Last Gentleman of the SAS* (Penguin, 2014).

Smith, Michael, *Station X – The Codebreakers of Bletchley Park* (Pan MacMillan, 2004).

Slader, John, *The Red Duster at War – The History of the Merchant Navy During the Second World War* (William Kimber and Co., 1988).

Webster, Charles, & Noble Frankland, *The Strategic Air Offensive Against Germany 1939–1945*, four volumes (Her Majesty's Stationery Office, 1961).

Self-Published Books

Rorke, Pat, *Every Common Bush* (Amazon Kindle, 2011).

Hooker, Fred, *Lest We Forget* (Advantage, 2012).

de Bernière-Smart, Major Piers, *'Golden Apples': The Poetry of Piers Alexander* (FCS Designworks, 2006).

Gerrard, Mady, Full Circle – A Story of Survival and Hope (Duncan Print Group, 2006).

Pulham Market Society, *Memories of Pulham Market – An Oral History of the Twentieth Century* (Postprint, 2007).

Pulham Market Society, *Memories of Wartime – Taken from Recordings Made by Local People* (Postprint, 2012).

Online Sources

http://www.bbc.co.uk/history/worldwars/wwtwo/ – various.

Royal Air Force Historical Society, *Journal 51* – for 5153 Squadron. https://www.rafmuseum.org.uk/documents/research/RAF-Historical-Society-Journals/Journal-51.pdf

Royal Air Force Squadron Histories – for 244, 102, 608 and 50 Squadrons.

Royal Air Force Bomber Command: https://www.rafbf.org/bomber-command-memorial/about-bomber-command

Portsmouth Naval Memorial: https://www.cwgc.org/find/
find-cemeteries-and-memorials/144703/portsmouth-naval-
memorial
http://www.historyofwar.org/articles/battles_lowestoft_raid.html
http://www.pulhamstmarypc.org.uk/history/royal-navy-air-
station/

Magazines

Aeromodeller, published by Doolittle Publishing (Chris Ottewell).

ACKNOWLEDGEMENTS

First and foremost, of course, my gratitude is for all who have opened their hearts and minds so that this book could be written. Thank you all for welcoming me into your homes and allowing me the privilege of listening to your memories.

My heartfelt dearest thanks, in the order for which they appear in *Remarkable Journeys of the Second World War*, to John Ottewell, Bill Carter, Pat Rorke, Douglas Huke, Fred Hooker, Piers de Bernière-Smart, Colin Bell, Mady Gerrard, Peter Blackburn, Dr Noble Frankland and Ray Edwards.

Thank you also to friends and family members who helped make the interviews possible: Chris Ottewell, Di Ford, Joss Sanglier, Pat Smith, Louis de Bernières, Charlotte Baker, Linda Frankland, Maggie and Hans Van Rij, Elizabeth Hooker, Alison Schwier, Mike Newby, Sarah Hague, Alex Blanshard, Nicola Shannon, Nick Jenkins, Tim Kiddell, Darren France, and Victoria Field.

Thank you, too, Graham Cowie and Harry Burgoyne for the many introductions they have given me through their work bringing the Second World War RAF veterans together each year at their annual Project Propeller gathering, at which I have always been made welcome.

Thank you, too, Christopher Hand and Sean Allerton for your careful proofreading.

Thank you, also, for all the endorsements and to Elizabeth Halls and James Bashall for their forewords. I am touched by these expressions of understanding about the weight of the words contained within this book.

Thanks to James Stephens at Biteback for confirming my use of the POW stories.

Thank you also to Andrew Hayward for being a wonderfully supportive agent, and to Amy Rigg and Alex Waite at The History Press for sharing with me the strength and vitality of these stories.

Finally, thank you to those closest to me who have undoubtedly been sometimes neglected as I have prioritised putting words on each page. My children, Rollo and Ranulph, brothers, Henry and Richard, and sister, Sarah and her family, thank you.

And to William Drew-Batty for the constancy of his encouragement and kindness. And also thank you to William for his music.